ITALIANS IN MY PAPER BAG

ITALIANS IN MY PAPER BAG

JILLIAN RICHARDS

EPIGRAPH BOOKS
RHINEBECK, NEW YORK

Paperback ISBN 978-1-954744-07-3
eBook ISBN 978-1-954744-08-0

Library of Congress Control Number 2021904016

Book design by Colin Rolfe

Epigraph Books
22 East Market Street, Suite 304
Rhinebeck, NY 12572
(845) 876-4861
epigraphps.com

I dedicate this book to my beloved sons Luke Benjamin Morey and Toby John Morey, who have loved me unstintingly and held me up with giving hands and gentle hearts.

Borders? I have never seen one. But I have heard they exist in the minds of some people.

—THOR HEYERDAHL

Jillian @ 33

HALF LIGHT

It cannot have been the milkman. I cannot believe it was the milkman!

Once upon a time there was a woman who had been named Annie Merle at birth. Her father's name was Francis Capuano, and at the time of Merle's birth he was forty-three years old. Her mother's name was Annie Miree, and she was thirty-nine years old at that time.

Annie Miree Matthews was the youngest of eight children born to Catherine Fitzpatrick and Richard Matthews. Catherine came from Clare, Ireland, and Richard was from Perthshire, in Scotland. Richard and Catherine married in Adelaide, South Australia, in 1850. They moved to Creswick, Victoria, a few years later. Catherine and Richard were my maternal great-grandparents.

Although she would not have told you had you met her, Annie Merle Capuano Pavarno Richards was my mother's long and complicated name, and with her life, as with her name, she carried forward the Italian dots and dashes of what was destined to become my genetic heritage. With that moniker, Merle was always "the Italian" in our family—or at least she was the *part Italian* in our family. She was a Capuano, after all.

That is, she was a Capuano until she found out that she was not, and was admonished severely by authorities for having had the audacity to believe all her life that Capuano was her rightful name. "They" told her in no uncertain terms that she was, in fact, a Pavarno. She was fifty-seven years of age at the time of this bombshell, and her whole sense of self was upended. She was tossed into a state of utter confusion at this shocking news. It was impossible for her to believe what she was hearing. What was it they were trying to tell her? How could such a thing be possible? Who did they say she was? What was it that they had said?

Having had no say whatsoever in her naming, she had inherited the moniker Capuano along with her genes. The genes and the name had traveled with her throughout her life, she not having given one iota of thought to them. Now *they* were demanding that she must depart from their august presence post haste, go back over her life with a fine-tooth comb, and consider with care who she really was. She must discover for herself whether she was a Capuano or a Pavarno, or whether she was perhaps both—or then again, perhaps neither. What if she was neither? It was beyond Merle's ability to think straight.

She never could have guessed the consequences of her seemingly simple application for her first passport. No one would have expected this turn of events. Up until now Merle was an ordinary, law-abiding, middle-aged woman living an ordinary life in an ordinary house in an ordinary suburb— driving an ordinary car, with ordinary friends and an ordinary dawg in the backyard. Nothing had prepared Merle for such a confrontation. As much as she scrambled to hold her dignity in check while in *their* presence, she felt much more inclined to sit down and weep when she returned to 45b. Was life around her to come to a devastating full stop again as it had when her mother had died? She was shocked into a quiver of indignation.

Had some person or persons deliberately deceived her all of her life? If so, who and why? Or could she in fact be the ill-conceived child of one of the local milkmen? That was a hard thing for a child left motherless at the age of eight to imagine, but could that be the reason why she could only describe her father to me as "an angry man"? What had happened behind the closed doors of their home in St. Kilda before the early demise of her dearly beloved mother—dead at the age of forty-eight after having given birth to seven children, two of whom grieved over and buried in their infancy? Was this a factor in the confusion? Merle had no capacity to deal with any of this. Who were these authorities that were ruining her equilibrium and threatening to ruin her travel plans and, in the process, ruining her sense of self by tossing at her ideas she could not begin to contemplate? They sat like statues with their bureaucratic noses in the air, supercilious and in charge, while she longed for somewhere to hide. "I always thought I was Merle Capuano," she whispered. "I was always told I was Merle Capuano. If I am not, who am I?" But no one answered, and into the silence crept fear, silent and cold as death. The safety net had gone. Merle would need to discover and then to grow into a whole new sense of self. This would take a lot of time and all of her courage. Confusion had been dropped into her lap, and it was far more than she could manage to contemplate.

A lot of conjecture and guesswork and a bit of gap-filling was needed to patch up this hole in Merle's bucket.

THERE'S A HOLE IN MY BUCKET

What a business is this trekking back and forth across the vast oceans of my family heritage. It has left me standing quietly by the window staring out as I fiddle with the scratchy little grains of sand that have stuck to my fingers, gathered up from the seemingly unconnected islands of confusing information upon which I stand immersed up to my ankles, tentatively searching around me for clues. At my feet lies the flotsam and jetsam of my rellies, washed up and bobbing around on the shores of my life. Most of them had lived through their own private worlds—not recording at all, not photographing much, and not doing much of anything except living as they crisscrossed this mortal coil, sending their whisperings down through the decades to me.

My son Toby John lives in the port city of Gothenburg in Sweden. It was there that he and his partner Linda Kristina brought their creative selves to bear as they contemplated purchasing a gift for my birthday. There it was that they decided a gift of a DNA test could offer me a breath of fresh inspiration. The kit would be mailed to me in place of the usual very welcome bottles of champagne or bundles of books. I was more than ready for a little light-hearted inspiration, as Covid-19 had been spewing its devilish breath out across the world and chasing our tails for far too many weeks. Covid-19 was intensely committed to a daring bid to entrap us all in its deathly grasp, and I found it galling to listen to the list of tragedies day after day after day as we hunkered down in Melbourne town—holding our breath with the rest of the world, watching and waiting for the inevitable daily count of death and destruction. An eerie hush hung over Melbourne town. An eerie hush hung over the world. We had all been brought to our knees. I was beginning to call it STIFUS-19 and wanting desperately to slap it away in fury and frustration.

When Toby said, "Time to explore the family secrets, Ma," with a dimpled grin, I had unwittingly jumped with both feet and without warning right into a big fat world of Italian trouble. His offer had made me happy.

In due course a small, plain-covered, secret-revealing package arrived in Melbourne town, addressed to me. There were no flashing red lights on the package and nothing at all warning me to open it with care. So open it, I did, and read through every single instruction. I had no reason to feel a sense of alarm. No threat seemed to be attached to that package either inside or out. I had no goose bumps and I felt no fear.

Following the instructions to the letter, I spat a little ladylike spittle into the vial, raced to the post office dodging COVID all the way, lined up wearing my mask and social-distancing, paid my dues, and sent it winging its way on its own little

DNA voyage into the Never-Never. I came home as excited as a school kid. "Perhaps I will learn something new," I thought.

TO EXIST

During my busy adult life, I had not taken time to do anything more about my family history than read the copious notes Willis had written regarding the Richards clan while trying to remember the few details Merle had ever let loose about her clan in my presence. I did know that there was Scottish heritage on both sides of my family as well as some British and some Irish, and I knew that my mother was of Italian descent, carrying the moniker Capuano for most of her life. But nothing prepared me for the fact that following in the train of that ladylike tittle of spittle from my mouth came a personal shock that would continue to reverberate even up until now. That shock tossed one big fat spaghetti-flavored mystery into the space that now surrounds the Italians in my paper bag of life. It hovers, smirking at me from the depths of the bag.

All fifty-seven years of Merle's life were lived as a Capuano until my (first) son Nathan David was born while I was living back East in the United States. Following a serious discussion and careful checking of their finances, Willis and Merle decided that, as family called, it was time for them to visit us in Salem, Massachusetts, where I was living in an apartment building that had previously been run as a brothel and that sat directly opposite the famous Witch House. A keen history buff, Willis prepared an extensive agenda so that we could enjoy the wealth of early American history together while he was with us.

We visited the Niagara Falls, the three magnificent falls straddling the border between the United States and Canada. There Willis paid to have two-inch banner headlines printed onto the front page of a newspaper, proclaiming to all who would read, "Willis Richards visits the Niagara Falls." I have that paper still and smile in acknowledgment at his self-depreciating humor as I think of it. We visited Independence Hall, where the Declaration of Independence was first adopted, and where the US Constitution was written. We visited the Plymouth Plantation and wandered the decks of the Mayflower II tall ship, a reproduction of the Mayflower that brought the Pilgrims to the New World in 1620. Willis was in his element, full sure that he knew more than any of the guides or latent historians who were offering information.

Willis had fought in Papua New Guinea and surrounding areas for three years during World War II, but Merle's life adventures had never carried her further north than Queensland or south to Tootgarook, where Willis had built a shack out of fossicked materials following his return from World War II. It was during the exciting process of applying for her first Australian passport for the purpose of visiting us in Salem that Merle discovered to her deep consternation that she did not exist. In that mandatory interview she was informed in no uncertain terms by the bureaucrats who hold sway over such things as our lives, "Yes, we can see you standing there in front of us, but you do not exist." "No, you do not!"

she was told to her quieter and more and more embarrassed protestation.

"But I do! I am," she tried to protest, pointing fearfully to herself. But no.

The Tootgarook shack built as a getaway by Willis from fossicked materials following his return from WW II. He called it: Our Weekender. I prefer Our Chalet, or even Our Dacha.

"The papers I have held here in my official hand tell me that there is no Anne Merle Capuano. No, there is not!" said the authorities, in chorus now with louder and louder voices. "You, so called Anne Merle Capuano Richards, do not exist. There is no such person. You are not registered. Not only may you not have a passport, but you had jolly well better hurry up and get in and visit those who will decide if you do exist, why you exist, and why you have not told us that up until this very minute you did not exist. Despite your having slept and eaten and married and given birth and pretended to be alive all these years, you do not exist!" This last, underlined in officialese as a loud interruption, came careening into Merle's and Willis's lives totally devoid of humor. Neither of them had had any reason to consider that there would be such an electrifying jolt following their applications for passports. This drama looked set to upend their highly anticipated travel.

There was suddenly the despairing thought that perhaps Merle had been fooled by far too many for far too long. It was hard for her to think. Her brow furrowed and a tear rolled slowly down her cheek. Was this a mere cul-de-sac, or was it some terrible new highway she must learn to navigate? Had someone pulled up the ladder behind her as she clambered her way through life? Was she not the fruit of those Italian loins after all? Had she played an unwitting part in any of this? If so, what was it? And what about the milkman? And could there have been more than one milkman?

The bureaucrat's head descended again to his papers and with it any euphoria regarding the proposed trip. Willis and Merle were dismissed. They were obstructed, and they had not yet begun. Officialdom can be daunting, and Merle had just been daunted into oblivion without any explanation. She was shocked and frightened.

It had become her responsibility to prove that she existed, and the burden thus placed on her womanly shoulders was almost more than she could bear. She did not know what to think any more than she knew how to think. As the days passed, Merle became increasingly worried that she might not take the planned trip of a lifetime, that she might not be able to visit us in Salem and meet her newest grandson. She worried about who they should see and what they should ask. This jolt was undermining her confidence and leaving her head in a curious place of disarray.

STATE OF VICTORIA

"NO RECORD" RESULT № 134607
JB

OFFICE OF THE GOVERNMENT STATIST

Melbourne, 16th April, 1970.

Re Application Fol. 187243

MEMO.

The Indexes of this office from 1/1/1911

to 31/12/1915 have been searched, but no record

can be found therein of the birth

of Anne Marie CAPUANO
on
alleged to have occurred in the year 6/1/1913

ANNE MERLE PAVARNO
DoB 6/1/1913
N 12-2712/69

Balaclava VIC.

MOTHER Annie MATTHEWS
FATHER Francis CAPUANO

V. H. ARNOLD
Government Statist

Merle's NO RECORD result.

It was fortunate for Merle that Willis had spent enough years dealing with officialdom in the Royal Australian Air Force to know a thing or two. He also knew a bloke or two. He gathered himself together and prepared to deal with Merle's moniker. By the time he had polished his medals and brought his shoes into line with a good spit and polish he was right back on the parade ground at Point Cook ready to assert himself. Willis stepped forward—chin up, eyes forward, and ready for action. "Backs to the wall," he would tell us in times of trouble, aware that it would come. Straighten up. Get on with it.

Merle sat herself down with a thump once they returned from that affronting visit to passport bureaucracy. She was unable to think, unable to cry, and unable to see how she could ever put herself back together again. She felt like a shrunken version of herself. How could she look anyone in the eye? What would people think? What would they say? There continued to be days of despair and disbelief exclusive to Merle.

She felt she was broken into pieces like the proverbial Humpty-Dumpty and in great need of all the king's horses and all the king's men to come to her aid. When she was a young girl learning to type, one of the exercises proposed by drill instructor Charles E. Weller was, "Now is the time for all good men to come to the aid of their party." At this moment in time the one good man Merle knew was Willis, and he assured her that he would help her far more than all the king's horses and all the king's men.

Willis went into battle. The daunting consequences of inaction propelled him onward and forward into time-consuming phone calls and visits to the registry of births, deaths, and marriages before all the traipsing and trudging back and forth to the city led to the unveiling of the truth behind Merle's "nonexistence." Willis had not quite been to war on Merle's behalf, but he knew instinctively that he had entered a battleground where he was fighting in the bureaucratic world of "those who know."

When the vital information was finally unearthed, Merle experienced a deeply felt personal relief, and with that, the rhythm of her breathing settled into a shallow in an out, in and out—pushing and pulling like the bellows before a fire. A newly colored world was opening up in front of her as she officially became known as Annie Merle Capuano Pavarno Richards. She adjusted her glasses and settled herself quietly on the floral couch. Her existence was now permitted. She had become the puzzled possessor of a new name, and she remained hoping quietly for the rest of her life that she really was who she said she was, even as there hovered close behind her a shadow of fear.

And they did travel to Salem, and they did meet Nathan David, and Willis did convince me to take him on every history jaunt we could fit in.

As I endeavored to sift and sort out this tale of confusion, I was aware that I was slowly being sifted and sorted out myself. Information in bits and pieces wafted into my life in the form of tired scraps of paper and in barely legible writing on the backs of old photographs that were brought out into the light of day.

I could not have imagined how much more detailed sifting and sorting of my own I would need as a result of sending my little package of ladylike spittle off for its genetic examination. I was preparing for a rendezvous with my own identity.

THERE'S SOMETHING ABOUT THAT NAME

Capuano refers to the Italian city of Capua that was located northeast of Naples in southern Italy. Capua was one of the oldest, biggest, richest, and most important cities in the ancient world. Italy's second-largest amphitheater was built there. It is also known to be where Spartacus started the Slave Revolt. A fortified city founded in about 600 BC, it was built on the site of the ancient city of Casilinum as one of the defenses of the kingdom of Naples and connected with Rome by the construction of the Via Apia in 312 BC. Capua enjoyed great prosperity until it was burned to the ground in AD 840. Its modern name is Santa Maria Capua Vetere.

It is said that persons bearing the Capuano family name were involved in important events in the early Kingdom of Naples and decorated with noble titles and knighthoods. I dare claim no pompous conclusions from this information since I am unable to establish who it was who said such. There is a reference to a Cardinal Peter of Capua, who reportedly brought the remains of Saint Andrew from Constantinople to Amalfi in 1208, whatever good that could possibly do me.

The confusion regarding the Capuano-Pavarno name harks back a generation or two, as far back as my great-grandfather "old Antonio," who departed the shores of the Greek Ionian island of Corfu in approximately 1839. Or possibly he departed Corsica. How will I ever be sure? It is said that he was

—

attracted by stories of vast gold discoveries in Victoria. Either way, he made his way on a ship on which his brother Michael was captain, crossing the vast oceans to the southern continent of Australia, *Terra Australis*. Once their ship reached safe harbor at the port of Geelong in Victoria, Antonio jumped ship and headed for the gold fields, walking, while his brother Michael sailed on to the new world of America, eventually returning to Corfu, where he lived out the rest of his life.

As a newly arrived "chum," Antonio's Italian accent would have been strong. Did bureaucrats waiting for disembarking immigrants write down his name in big books, doing their best to spell it out as it sounded to them? What did they write? Was Antonio able to read or to write himself? Could he have checked what they wrote? Names mispronounced can be the cause of disproportionate offence, and names misspelled continue be a cause of misunderstanding. My best guess is that at the birth of the confusion regarding the family name of Capuano-Pavarno, diligent recorders of names of immigrants arriving in Australia from all over the world both misheard and misspelled them.

One historian has found our particular family name to be spelled as *Pavarno* on Antonio's marriage certificate, then later crossed out on the same marriage certificate and rewritten as *Capuano*. No one had the decency to leave me a note telling me why that change. Neither did they leave a note for Merle or any other family member I have ever met. A distant Capuano relative researched the family name in Australia and found it to be spelled variously over the years as: Pavans, Pavino, Pavrono,

Paurono, Paurwo, Pavano, Parvano, Pavarno, Pevano, Pevino, Pervano—then Capuano: Capuans, Capauano, Capararo, Capanno, Capouno, and Capuano. That research must have caused a furrow or two to crease her womanly brow. It is enough to give this girl a headache.

I have learned to my great relief that across the pond in New Zealand the cousins are all still known as Pavarno and have never been known as Capuano. Smart, those New Zealanders.

Friends confide similarly complex stories concerning their family names. Some laugh as they recall their first days in Australia. Some are still grieved. One Egyptian friend told me that his name was Fred, which puzzled me. It did not sound Egyptian to my ears. "Oh yes, it is," he assured me, smiling so broadly that his thatch of thickly bristled black moustache stretched across his beautiful face from one ear to the other.

"Tell me about that," I asked, all ears. "I was told this by a man on the tram I took to find work on my second day in Australia." *Oh really, I grimaced to myself.* "Oh yes," he grinned, pleased with his tale. "He asked me for my name, and I told him, Bomani. It means warrior. I liked my name." He smiled ruefully. "So, why Fred?" I pressed. "He was a very kind man," he went on. "He told me that in Australia I would be called Fred." For as long as I have known this gentleman, he has been called Fred, and it pains me every time I hear it. My grief for him spilled over when he went on with his tale, telling me that his brother also came to live in Australia and also met an Aussie bloke on a tram. He has been known ever since by the name Fred. Were those Aussie blokes on trams one and the same? And were they joking and then misunderstood by the newly arrived Egyptians? Or was it that they could not be bothered to attempt the correct pronunciation?

How much grief can follow the misuse of our primary sense of self, a given name. Even in this, our twenty-first century, a note regarding visa applications for Australia states that, "Entering names incorrectly may result in denial of permission to board an aircraft to Australia, or result in delays in border processing on arrival to Australia, even if the applicant has been granted a visa."

ME NO UNDERSTAND

It was not only Antonio who ran slap-bang into a sticky spiderweb of trouble with his unexpected accent. Passports safely in hand, Willis and Merle finally arrived in Massachusetts to visit with us and meet Nathan David. Willis was bent on being generous in many ways. Possessed of a lifelong sweet tooth, he was quick to sniff out the best offerings in Salem, panting to indulge himself in the buying of sweetmeats from the local bakery in order to share them with us and with our neighbors. But his dreams quickly turned to reality. He ran into trouble as soon as he opened his mouth. Those who came to the counter smiling their charm and willingness to serve him could not understand one single word he said. He sounded strange to them, foreign even, and their widened eyes and their muffled laughter showed it. Not a man to be easily daunted, Willis tried and tried, and then tried again but was unable to give way to their Massachusetts accent—and they were neither able nor willing to understand his broad Aussie one. They shuffled their feet behind the counter in agitation as their polite New England ways turned to gentle mirth, finally bursting out into laughter.

A small Aussie flag in Nathan's hand in a photograph with Willis is a precious reminder of those fleeting moments.

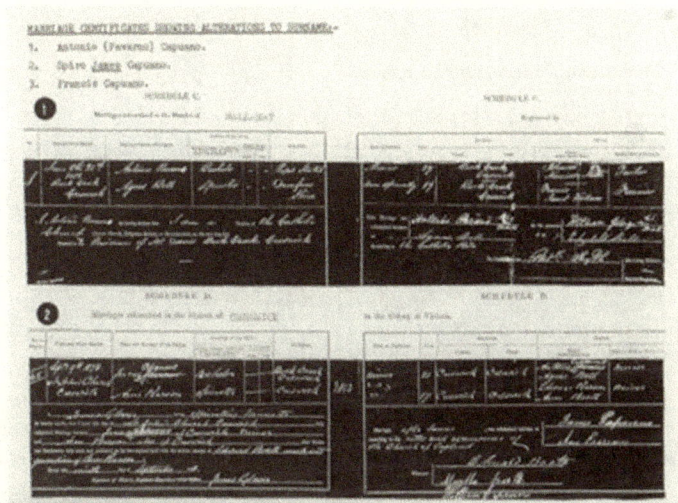

Marriage certificates showing alterations to surnames.

I, Anne Merle Richards of 45B Bowen Street, Chadstone, Victoria, do

that to the best of my knowledge, belief, and assurances received, I was born to Francis Pavarno (father) and Annie Pavarno (mother) nee Matthews at St. Kilda, Victoria on the 6th January, 1913. I was named Anne Merle Pavarno. Shortly after my birth my father changed his and my surname to Capuano, and this surname is the only surname I was known by until my marriage. At all times I understood the change of name of my father and self to be by Deed Poll.

A recent check by the Government Statist produced a NO RECORD result of the birth of Anne Merle Capuano on the 6th January, 1913, but confirmed the birth of Anne Merle Pavarno on that date (see attached). A check with the Registrar Generals Office has revealed no legal change of name by Deed Poll.

Merle's Statutory Declaration in regard to her name. Even this looks confused.

Undaunted by what he perceived as rudeness, Willis kept at it, getting louder and louder in the vain hope that volume would solve his problem. It did not. All he could feel was surprise at the slap of frustration landing heavy and cold on his gesticulating hand. The reality of the situation was beyond him, and all of his pointing and his loud voice had done nothing to clarify it. Those serving behind the counter looked at each other now, not resorting to the suppression of effrontery but giggling helplessly behind their hands until I was forced to intervene and interpret Willis's generous desires into my best Americanese. Peace was restored and Willis shuffled off with his bags of goodies to share with any who were friendly enough to engage in conversation with him. That made him happy.

He turned to me in confusion and surprise as he expressed his concern and disbelief at the ignorant and inarticulate ways of New Englanders. Willis had found them disturbing.

A JOT AND TITTLE

On and on and on rolled my disbelief as I gazed at my DNA results. I felt appalled and affronted. "This has to be a mistake. There is not one reference to Italian genes? That cannot be right. They cannot be right. Their systems must be off," I fumed and fussed to myself as I paced and stamped and generally behaved like a small child in the throes of a tantrum.

Couldn't one of the brilliant people in DNA-heaven be smart enough to have conjured up one drip of my Italian heritage, the one drip that would make me feel more like the "me" I had thought I had known all of my life? I did not really have a preference—either a drip or a drop would suffice. By now, my initial excitement at the gift of DNA analysis for my birthday was beginning to melt into insignificance behind my upheld hands, hiding itself in horror and shame, embarrassment and disbelief. I felt as daunted as Merle must have done when she was told that she did not exist. As much as I had loved the gifts of books and champagne delivered right to my Melbourne doorstep from the Swedish family over the past few years, a DNA test had sounded perfect for my birthday this time.

My daughter-in-law Linda Kristina had recently subjected herself to a DNA test, and having believed that she was of pure Swedish stock had been more than a little surprised to discover that a drop or two of British DNA had crept in very quietly and while no one was looking a generation or two before. Toby John had learned about his heritage from chatter at family gatherings, although he had not yet submitted himself to a DNA test. Despite this, he had been permitted to live and work in the United Kingdom for a few years when his research had determined that his paternal grandmother had been born there. He knew that Willis and Eddie had reveled in their study of one branch of the Richards family history for fifteen years and had established firmly that the Richardses were composed of a wondrous cocktail of Irish, English, and Scottish blood. From Merle's side he knew there had always been the Italian connection mixed with a drop or two of Scottish blood.

As I began to reflect on all this mixing and matching, I was reminded that I had a set of cookbooks written by a New England cook who admonished her students that not one scrap of food should ever be wasted. She admonished them that any leftover soup could and should be used in the making of gravy. Not satisfied with that, however, she went on to admonish them to remember that the leftover gravy could and should be used in the making of soup. I can conclude without any reservation that my family is just like that soup and we are also just like that gravy, mixing and matching generation after generation. Not one scrap is wasted.

Merle grew through her childhood years during the grotesque horrors of World War I bearing the surname Capuano. Italians were not well regarded in Australia at that time, mostly because of Mussolini and his doings, and this left her moving into her young adult life with a somewhat defensive view of her name. But it remained present nevertheless, breathing its way through her childhood and then on through mine. "Capuano. Capuano." One Capuano gentleman I met declared with some pleasure that he was my cousin and therefore he considered us close, even though he was ten years older than I and I hardly knew him. Another Capuano was an Australian footballer of some note whose name would appear in Melbourne newspapers from time to time. This would lead to one of the distant rellies pointing to the article and looking inordinately proud, as though it were they who were famous just by their attachment to the name.

Willis was like all members of the Richards clan, loquacious. They did not so much gossip as tell stories about themselves. These were often tall or exaggerated tales with a ridiculously funny twist. The Irish kissing of the Blarney Stone endows the kisser with the gift of gab and this was evident in all of them. The word *blarney* means "clever, flattering, or coaxing talk." And were they good at that.

Merle remained unusually silent regarding her family tales. My maternal grandparents had died before I was born. Merle's father, Francis Capuano, had died when Merle was three-months pregnant with me and while Willis was away fighting in New Guinea attempting to the keep the threat of a Japanese invasion of Australia at bay. It was not Merle who told me this, or even Willis. I discovered it myself when I went on my family history hunt. This was to become the first of many surprises. The surprises ultimately became of such import that I was sent scrambling to gather myself together in order to comprehend why none of this had ever been discussed in my presence, even in clandestine whispers.

I was well into my family history hunt when I discovered for the first time that Merle was the youngest of seven siblings. Seven? Even *that* was news. I had met her eldest brother, Francis Clifford Richard Matthew Pavarno, at various family gatherings when I was a child, but never once was his family name of Pavarno discussed in relationship to Merle's. Neither were the names of the other siblings who remain a total mystery until this day. I have vague memories of my Uncle Cliff as a tall, quiet man who worked at the Myer Emporium. His wife was my Auntie Babs, who carried her strong Scottish brogue with her to the grave, as did many in Australia at that time. Babs exuded a Scottish sense of bustle that was only barely held in check under her tightly fitted suits, and she remembered to send me a lace-edged handkerchief every birthday for years. There were two Pavarno daughters of theirs, my first cousins, whom I met once or twice before they disappeared out of my life. Clifford remained a Pavarno until the day he died, and no one that I ever met questioned the fact that he and Merle carried different surnames.

As I grew into adulthood I slowly began to puzzle away and ponder as to why it was that Francis Clifford Richard Matthew was a Pavarno, and his youngest sister, Merle, was Annie Merle Capuano. It was mysterious, as my Parisian friend Monsieur Polio would say.

I was puzzled but not much troubled at that time, as I was well occupied with a multitude of things to do—moving countries, moving houses, raising babes, working to put a man through two masters degrees, and moving house again and again and again. But I did puzzle away quietly in whichever corner of the world I was living at the time.

Uncle Cliff: Francis Clifford Richard Matthew Pavarno

And then one day it came to pass that further mysteries began to pop up in and around "the Italian bit" of the family in my paper bag of life.

OVER THE SEA TO MASSACHUSETTS

When Willis and Merle decided to pack up their kit bags and travel halfway around the world to visit us in Salem, Massachusetts, it was to be a major adventure for them both. Off they had scurried to have their passports prepared. These they would have ready to grasp in their nervous hands as they trudged in and out of airports on their way across the world from Melbourne to Salem.

Merle had been shocked into incomprehension at the result of the initial mandatory passport interview, as Willis had been. Who was it that he had married all those years ago? Were the two of them indeed legally married? As I learned of their conundrum, it became not just Merle who was shocked. I was surprised and shocked too. "Who am I?" I began to think as I jockeyed my way through my own history. "And who was *she*?"

There was Merle, case packed, hair permed, Aussie flag at the ready—and she was stuck to the ground. Nailed down tight. "No, Merle. Sorry. No, madam. You do not exist," she was informed. Her conundrum was deeply personal. The paper work that went back and forth, the telephone calls and the numerous nervous visits to officialdom can only be imagined. Merle was flummoxed enough already at the idea of overseas travel, let alone being confronted with her nonexistence. No one had ever asked her to prove that she was alive before. Somewhere between the birth of her eldest brother, Francis Clifford Richard Matthew Pavarno, and her birth it had been decided that she would be a Capuano. Who had decided? When had they decided? Why had they decided? Up until this it had not caused her to puzzle. But then Merle was not one for much puzzling of any kind.

I was the one who started to puzzle away as I moved into my family tale.

While Willis and his kin had gossiped and laughed at the family table, they had also filled us to the brim with of the stories of their lives. "Remember when …" would leave a lilting breath of silence until they moved rapidly on into banter and interruption, laughter and side-slapping, arguing and giggling as they gossiped about where they lived out their youth "up the road from the Kelly gang," or on a dray on the way to the local hall for a Saturday night dance, or evading the cruelty of the "old rascal" of a schoolmaster at Wilby school, or chanting out Australian poetry to the beat of a drum, or working like "bullockies" on the farm.

But Merle? Where were her tales? Where was her childhood? Where was the stuff of legend that I thought made up all families?

ANCESTORS

My maternal grandfather, Francis Capuano Pavarno, died at the age of seventy-two. He was the seventh of the eight children of Antonio Capuano Pavarno, an Italian, and Agnes Little Bell, a Scot.

Their eldest son, my granduncle Spiro James Capuano, and his wife, Anne Pearson, produced seventeen children. Their second son, Antonio William Capuano, and his wife produced eight children. Their third son, Christopher Henry Capuano, died at three months. Their fourth son, John Henry Capuano, and his wife produced nine children. Their fifth child was a girl, Agnes Jane Capuano, who had no children. The sixth child was also a girl, Elizabeth Enunciate (Hettie) Capuano. She and her husband produced four children. Following my grandfather, another boy child was born and named Johannah Harknes Capuano. He died at five months.

I can think of nothing to add. No wonder we ended up as a tribe of eight hundred and more in a few decades.

Annie Merle Capuano Pavarno Richards, my mother.

26

```
FRANCIS CAPUANO
B:16/ 7/1870 Bloody Gully,Cres.
D:17/ 6/1942 Melbourne
M1:28/ 3/1894 Creswick
ANNIE MARIE MATTHEWS
B:16/ 6/1873 Ascot
D: 9/ 4/1921 Melbourne
(Seven Children)
M2:13/10/1923 Brighton
ISABELLA McGREGOR MURCHIE
B:--/--/1891 Darvel,Scotland
D:18/ 7/1972 Melbourne
```

Francis Capuano Pavarno, my maternal grandfather.

TYKES AND OTHERS

In the Melbourne suburb where I stumbled through my childhood there were local legends about various families hither and yon and round about us on Bowen Street. There were fine neighbors whom Willis occasionally laughingly called "Tykes," which literally means "an unpleasant or coarse man." At that time the term was commonly used to refer to Roman Catholics, possibly because many had Irish heritage. These folk looked normal and behaved normally as far as I could see, and their children were my friends and neighbors whose parents I respected and liked. But I was warned not to allow my friendships to become too close, as *they* attended Mass and had ministers whom they called priests. They were *Roman Catholics*, of all things. Willis emphasized the *Roman* with a sense of arrogance and unjustified prejudice. He was a gregarious and generous-hearted man, but when religiosity rather than godliness got the better of him, he became rigid, autocratic, and unyielding. I did not like it.

If I looked across the hill to the far side of the verdant paddock where we scavenged for dinner-plate-sized mushrooms to be sautéed in butter for breakfast, there rose as an eruption a forbidding looking convent. Fortressing the convent there towered a monumental stone wall, along the top of which were jammed spikey chunks of glass that had been aggressively pushed down into concrete. Willis said the glass was jammed there in order that the nuns would never be able to escape. This was another puzzle for me, and I wondered what it was they might wish to escape from. We rarely saw these nuns, and I always felt sad that they were imprisoned so. Willis sounded sympathetic, but the convent and its stories frightened me. He also showed me a book that he had found in some odd bookshop entitled, *I Leapt Over the Wall*. This was not offered for me to read, but Willis intimated that it held dark secrets such as those that were hidden deep within the walls of our local convent.

All these years later I find out that Monica Baldwin's book is still in print. In it she said that she was no more fitted to be a nun than to be an acrobat. After reading that, I wished I had met her. Twenty-eight years of consecrated life was enough for Monica and she requested dispensation from her religious vows. Once removed from convent life, she was confronted by fashions, politics, and art—to which she needed to adjust. And there it is again, "Adjust simply, or simply adjust." Her book is considered a classic. But I am left still feeling anguish as I mentally contemplate the broken-glass-studded walls of the convent up the hill from 45b.

All these tales carried with them such a powerful sense of conspiratorial foreboding that I was caused to steer clear of venturing inside any Roman Catholic Church for a sneak peek for years. That is, until I went to work with the Sisters of Charity in Chicago, when the unseen barriers erected in my mind began to be pushed over by the gentle hand of a gracious God. And I melted to my knees in gratitude.

MOTHER DEAREST

Throughout all the years of my childhood Merle told me nothing much about herself except for the fact that she liked sewing when she was in school. And that she despised her stepmother, Isabella McGregor Murchie Capuano Pavarno. This latter she told me in a loud voice, but without words. Even as a child I could smell it. What had happened between them I did not know until an elderly friend of the family told me in confidence that Anne Merle and Isabella McGregor Murchie Capuano Pavarno had many terrible fights. This friend must have looked at my pale little Jillian face and thought that I needed some information in order to garner a little understanding of my own life. She did not elaborate, and to this day that is the only information I have about life in the childhood home of the Merle who all her life saw herself as alone in the world. The fact is that Merle did not tell me anything much about anything. There was nothing I could do about that. I felt no stab of frustration. I did not know what I did not know.

Despite Merle's obvious antagonism toward her, my sister Anne Miree and I had both loved Isabella, whom we called Nana Capp. I always felt that she loved us. When it was our turn to go to her Elsternwick home for a Sunday lunch after church, it was not the traditional Australian roasted lamb and vegetables we looked forward to with mouths watering, but Scottish fare: salt cod cooked with a marvelous white sauce and served with silken mashed potatoes. We loved it so that my mouth waters at the thought of it. For dessert we were graced with the world's best sago plum pudding topped with homemade custard and whipped cream. Each bite tasted of love.

Isabella McGregor Murchie Capuano Pavarno, my step-grandmother Nana Capp, and Francis Capuano Pavarno, my half-Italian grandfather who died before I was born.

What happened to Merle's tales? Although she lived until she was eighty years old, she spoke to me only once of her father, and that was when I had the raised the courage to ask her to, "Tell me about your father," as I was halfway out the door. "He was an angry man!" she spat out. And I bolted. And that, as they say, was that. Nothing else. She died with her tales enshrouded inside her.

Of her mother, who had died when Merle was eight years old, she spoke little and always with sadness—for Annie Marie Matthews Capuano Pavarno was the sweetest, loveli-est, kindest, and gentlest of mothers. I am sorry I was unable to know this grandmother. My Auntie Dell, Merle's older sister Madeline Catherine Adele, who was fourteen years older than Merle, intimated that she had similar memories and was moved to take a motherly interest in Merle for the rest of her life.

So I went a-hunting, and what I found sent me into a place of deep quietness.

In a photo I have of maternal grandmother Annie Marie Matthews, she is standing in repose as a bride on the verge of a new life with Francis Capuano, who is nowhere to be seen. How they met I do not know. How she felt I do not know. How he felt I do not know. Did she love this man she was about to marry? Did she want to marry him, or was this an arranged event? How long had they known each other? Did he want to marry her? Did he love her? I have no way of knowing and never will. I have no diary and no love letters tied with a ribbon and stored in lavender. I have no memento at all apart from this one solitary photograph.

I grew up aware of only two of the six siblings of Merle's. They were Francis Clifford Richard Matthew Pavarno and Madeline Catherine Adele, the eldest two. Now, so many years later, my research shocks me with the revelation that there was another girl child born to Francis Capuano Pavarno and Annie Marie Matthews, but the poor little babe's life-force ebbed away until she died at the tender age of three months. This babe was named Annie Merle too. As I read this I am horrified, frightened even. They named my mother, who was their youngest child, for a dead sibling? How could they? What a terrible burden for any young girl to bear. Did Merle ever know about this babe? I never once heard mention of the first Annie Merle either in sorrow or even in whispers. Following the brief life of the first Annie Merle, a boy child was born and duly named Francis Harold. My grandfather Francis Capuano Pavarno was certainly determined that he would be remembered one way or another with two of his male progeny named for him.

Then, and by this time I was almost on my knees, another girl child was born to them. She is recorded as "unnamed female." Ouch. This poor little scrap of humanity was not even named. Was Annie Marie's grief too great? Did Francis not care? This tiny bundle of life breathed her last after living for only one day. Did my mother know this? Was this too much for her to bear also? Is this why she never spoke of it? Or did no one ever tell her or whisper it where she heard. Did she follow in the train of the unspoken grief as she worked her way through life?

Following that, another male child was born and named John Henry. I never did meet either Francis Harold or John Henry, but as I grew older Willis told me in confidence and away from Merle's hearing that he had had to take care of their affairs when they died. Had he always known of their existence and had not told us? Or did he only find out upon their deaths? Why was he responsible to take care of their affairs? Did they ever marry? Were there children? Why was it that neither my Auntie Dell nor Merle ever mentioned them even once? They were my uncles, and I knew nothing of their existence until after their deaths. Why?

MOTHERLESS CHILD

As these stories of the Capuano-Pavarno family started to tumble into my life I felt an almost overwhelming compassion for Merle for the first time. There she was—a mere babe not yet on the edge of adulthood, fourteen years younger than her closest sibling, Adele—when her "sweet, beautiful, gentle" mother up and died. She was a little girl of eight years old and would now be stuck at home alone with a grieving and impossibly grumpy father. What had his life been like with the birth of seven children of his own and the death of two of them in infancy? His wife must have been both physically and emotionally exhausted after birthing so many babes and burying two. Perhaps he was also physically and emotionally exhausted. He was stuck in a place he could never have imagined. And eight-year-old Merle was stuck beside him.

So much more of Merle's personally felt anguish was revealed to me on one of my return trips from the United States to visit the family. I had brought Willis and Merle up to Sydney from Melbourne and made plans to take them with me to enjoy the opera at the Sydney Opera House. This was to be a special treat for Merle, who loved music and listened and sang along with the divine Maria Callas, who came right into our living room at 45b via the radiogram on Saturday nights.

We were preparing to fully enjoy the treat, dressed to kill

in our glad rags as we drove over the Sydney Harbor Bridge to join the throng at the spectacular Jorn Utzon-designed Opera House. I could name the spot where we were as I drove across the Sydney Harbor Bridge that night, although I cannot remember what led us into such an explosively revealing conversation. The evening light was glittering its reflections on the water of the harbor below us. The entrance to the city of Sydney is always triumphant, and we were dressed up and ready to join the city's chorus of praise to beauty and joy.

CHILLED

Without a smile anywhere near her voice, into this moment of pleasure Merle dropped words that chilled me into wordlessness. These words reverberated around the inside of my car, crashing into our night of joy without preamble.

I was totally unprepared. Willis must have been unprepared also. Suddenly into the joy of our anticipation in a quiet but determined voice, Merle dropped, "They took me in to see my mother when she died. Then I knew I was alone in the world, and I have been alone ever since." I was stunned into a loud silence. I could barely continue to drive. Traffic whizzed past me bleating its complaint as I involuntarily took my foot from the pedal. Willis was seated behind me and I could feel rather than see him draw in a sharp breath of astonishment. Merle had not cultivated our emotions or hers. And now she who did not normally reveal anything about her internal life was revealing the deepest alienation a child can feel.

Motherlessness. These words must have been coiled inside her for decades. Such a depth of feeling blundered drunkenly, across that small space from the back seat where she sat, to me at the wheel, that I felt as though I had been struck hard on the back of my neck. I felt Willis stiffen.

But she surely was wrong? Willis was sitting in front of her as we drove across the Sydney Harbor Bridge, admiring the panoramic view of the harbor, and they had been married for decades. I was sitting behind the wheel driving toward the spectacular Sydney Opera House, endeavoring to offer the best gift I could while they were with me in Sydney. And into this moment of shared joy Merle was stating out of the blue, emphatically and without preamble, that she was "alone in the world"? Did Willis and I not count?

She had been a prisoner of her own silence for far too long, and from somewhere far in the past I could hear the sound of her childish whimpers. She was revealing some of the contents of her heart and mind.

With trepidation I put my foot to the pedal, endeavoring to concentrate on the traffic and the curving road in front of me. I gathered myself and began to drive forward even as all my instincts were to stop the car, pull her out, and demand to know what she meant by such a bold statement. I wanted to yell at her. Could no one make up for the loss of her mother? I had not known that I needed to try. We—Wills and I—had not known that we needed to try.

I was now forced to reckon with the fact that it is impossible to give into a place where what you offer is not ever going to make up for loss, and that it is impossible to receive love if you have made a decision that you are alone. But, "alone in the world"? She was not, surely. But her felt need was so powerful that it takes my breath away as I think about it so many years later. It was a painful and severe confrontation.

Merle was stuck mid-sentence in her life with her feet nailed tight to the floor, a grieving eight-year-old girl with an Italian name, a motherless child. From that moment of drama, I began to understand why I have no memories of her holding my hand or kissing away my tears. I had not thought to miss that which I had never experienced. Merle remained stuck for the rest of her life, her felt needs bottled up inside and any possibility of a fully-lived life buried behind a mask of good clothes and appropriate friends, roast lamb on Sundays, and holidays at Tootgarook.

But the little I had known of Merle was vastly expanded. The whole shebang was hurled up onto the big screen of my mind, blasting it with bright lights and big, bold, brightly colored letters yelling at me.

Anne Marie Capuano Pavarno, Merle's "Dear Mother." I do not know where her father was.

PART ITALIAN

Despite such a profound lack of information from my mother, the one thing I was certain of was that I was part Italian. I had never been given any cause to doubt that. It became a bit of a "thing" of pride and quiet fun for Anne Miree and me as we shuffled our way through a limited and less-than-happy childhood. We took the Italian bit to ourselves with a tilt of our heads as though a little of the Italian glory story had rubbed off on us. If they were known for their good looks and sense of style, why could we not claim the same? In Australia the descendants of Antonio Capuano and his Scottish bride Agnes Little Bell had reproduced continuously until they numbered approximately eight hundred by the year 1990, and Anne Miree and I were two of that number. We had been born into a tribe that had scattered far and wide across the face of the earth like the children of Israel, and the Italian diaspora that had scattered were continuing to spread out and across this vast southern land of Australia.

LEAVING DARVEL

The year was approximately 1920. From the small town of Darvel in Scotland came one Isabella McGregor Murchie on the challenging journey to Australia. Her occupation was listed as "dressmaker." And somehow, somewhere, someday, Isabella met Francis. And at that meeting Isabella and Francis

Capuano Pavarno connected in some way, somehow. And they married—somehow, somewhere, and in some way.

From this distance it all seems implausible and improbable, if not impossible and definitely unlikely, although I have been assured that it did happen. I have succumbed to this tale because I have learned a tad about the surprises and impossibilities we all meet along our well-worn paths through life.

The small town of Darvel in Ayrshire, Scotland, is sometimes referred to as "the *Lang Toon*" (the Long Town). Lace was exported from the Darvel mills by the late-nineteenth century, as well as muslin and madras. Eventually, Darvel became known as "the Lace Town" and was ultimately known throughout the world for its lace. Lace curtains were said to have hung in most windows in Darvel. Roman settlements have been found there, and a battle between Robert the Bruce and the English was fought there on 10 May 1307.

The average temperature is recorded as a chilly 16.4 degrees Celsius (or 61.5 degrees Fahrenheit), even in mid-summer. It could have been that it was enough years of suffering with this chill that caused Isabella to up sticks and rush off to Australia. Despite the warmer climes of Australia, Isabella missed Scotland, and I remember that for many a year she devoured a Scottish newspaper received from a good friend she had left behind.

Isabella was to become my step-grandmother, but none of her Scottish burr with its uvular trill was to be part of my inheritance. She did however leave me memories of her love. She also left me a set of silver soupspoons in her will.

Isabella's birth certificate.

TO EXIST

As I waited impatiently for the results of my DNA test, I was in no way expecting to be stunned and flabbergasted into frustration. What is it that they mean by their determinations? How was it that *they* were so uninformed they could not even run a chook raffle? Was there some sly mix-up in the faraway kingdom of DNA? Or had they dropped my spittle and with one quick move substituted their own while no one was looking?

The shocking news they sent me felt far too much like a treacherous repeat of the dramatic situation where Merle had stood trembling in front of the authorities after she had been told that she did not exist. Now *they* were telling me with their jabbing fingers pointing to many maps and multitudinous dotted lines, and with a few tersely printed words, that my Italian heritage did not exist? No matter what I had been told up until now, it was not true. No matter that what I had supposed to be true was not true. This "Italian bit" was not mine. I could not claim it. I could not own it. I could not be proud of it. I could not speak about it. Did this mean that those Italians I had always thought were in my paper bag of life were not there at all and never had been?

As I pondered and fumed, paced the floor and raised my prayers to the heavens, I slowly changed my mindset and even checked myself in the mirror as I began to smile, secretly thinking to myself how furious this revelation would make my sister Anne Miree. Italy, she felt sure, was home. Each time her plane landed on Italian soil she would breathe in contentment, and peering out of the window would exclaim, "I'm home again!" On each visit to Italy, she smooched up to any Italian man she could catch by the tail, patted her cheek flirtatiously, tossed her black hair, and crooned, "Mama Italiano!"—nodding energetically as she preened to show that she was one of them and as good as they, and as creative and competent as any of them. She even shocked me into submission when she went so far as to offer me her most determined piece of sisterly advice. I told her that I had been working for many months with a brilliant Italian sculptor and artist. She was thrilled with that news. Turning to me, her eyes wide with pleasure, she leaned in close. "Marry him!" she admonished, "then he can buy a home in Italy, and we can all come and stay." With that she sat back in triumph. She had meant it. Good heavens, she was and continues to be irresistibly cheeky.

But the DNA-gurus I had consulted while I was still all wide-eyed and innocent insisted in loud voice that there was no Italian DNA to be found, at least not in my little bit of ladylike spittle. Now my reading and researching and trying to think and trying to remember continued into day-after-night-after-day. Moved into determined sleuthing, I began to write down family names and possible relationships as I remembered them, and I poked around in the deep recesses of my cupboards to find and bring to the light of day the tatty old black file box with its messy scraps of information and photographs that I had carried with me for years as I trekked my way back and forth across the world. After a few days of scrutinizing every scrap, I had no choice but to acknowledge that no matter how I calculated or how I tried to reckon it, at the very best, I could only be two-sixteenths Italian. Rats! I was hardly Italian at all. In that Italian part of my genome was a mere crumb—a morsel, if that—a mere tiny little tittle. Perhaps that morsel was embedded somewhere in my left hand, or in my right leg, or possibly in one of my breasts. Is that where the elusive DNA was hidden? Or was it hiding under my pillow, or perhaps under my bed? It was time for me to take a good look.

I began to recognize that it was the Italian name Capuano-Pavarno that had stuck to me like glue, distorting the truth. I had either been wearing the wrong glasses for far too long, or they were upside down. Was this naiveté, nostalgia, or simple fantasy? But I could not let it go easily, I still wanted my two-sixteenths of Italian DNA to be traceable, and *they* had told me it was not. It made me mad. How dare they do this to me? "Strike me pink!"—as older Australians would say.

My calmly competent older son, Luke, was at his gently reassuring best when he comforted me with, "Testing muddies the waters, Ma." He was all sympathy and repressed mirth. "It is not an exact science, Ma." Not exact. But not a drip? I did not exist? At least the Italian part of me did not exist? Where had it gone? Did it flee while I was traveling across the world? Did it get lost while I was scrambling around, mesmerized, in Machu Picchu, Peru—or when I poked one foot under the flimsy chain-link wire fence that created the border between Norway and Russia—or when I was walking in wonder along the Great Wall of China? Had it felt imprisoned like the nun and escaped over the wall, then over the hill and far away?

Who am I? Could not all those Pavarnos or Capuanos or Capuano-Pavarnos—or whoever they were—not leave me with one traceable drip of Italian to cling to? Something had gone terribly wrong in my paper bag of life. There was a hole in my bucket and all of my Italian-self appeared to have leached out.

Would it have remained with me, cozied up and safe, had I not subjected myself to that DNA test I had been so excited to take? How could all those Italians lurking about in the shadows of my life hang me out to dry like this? But they all had died before even one of them had the grace to tell me. And all that I had left to cling to was the fact that Merle was Italian, after all. Or was she? She was a Capuano, or perhaps she was a Pavarno, or perhaps she was both. Or perhaps she was neither.

That by itself was quite enough complexity for me. She looked as though she could have been Italian, once. I was impelled to settle back down with a glass of the best Chianti, slow my breathing to a walking pace and recognize that it really was my grandfather Francis Capuano who was the only true Italian in the past few generations. He certainly does look the part, or did, for—as he had the temerity to die before I was born—I was never able to sit on his knee, gaze into his face, and ask penetrating childish questions. But a name like Francis Capuano or Pavarno or Capuano-Pavarno was surely worth *something*.

Until I looked more closely and was caused to sink a little lower into myself, my Italian fantasies were slowly sinking into the earth like a grave, as Willis would say. It was not Francis, but his father and my great-grandfather Antonio Capuano (or Pavarno, or Capuano-Pavarno) who was *the Italian*. He was the one—from Corfu, or Corsica, or from wherever he came—who sailed away one summer's day to become "the beginning of the Capuano family in Australia." From his loins had come a quiver full of eight hundred or more rellies in Australia, all carrying the same moniker. And I was one of them. *And I was not Italian?* I was flummoxed.

It would hardly be fair for me to call Sweden to ask Linda and Toby to pay for another DNA test. None of this was their fault. They were offering me only kindness. When they huddled away in Sweden and used their combined intelligence and love and their threads of heritage of the Swedish, Danish, Norwegian, English, Scottish, and Italian kind to enhance my life with my first DNA test, it had seemed to be a very good plan.

Now I would have to swallow my pride but not my spittle. I would have to spit one more time into a little tube and send it winging its way to DNA-heaven or wherever DNA samples go, and wait with baited breath until *they* took their time and got it right. (Sounds a bit like The Donald on election night in the USA.)

And while I pondered and paced, I recognized I also felt somewhat miffed that I would have to pay for the DNA-guru's disturbance of my equilibrium one more time.

My sanity now hung precariously in the balance.

IT'S NOT EASY BEING GREEN

I looked in despair and with a deal of quiet ladylike swearing at the garden clippings I had chopped and dropped into the green bin for recycling. The realization had dawned on me that green clippings go into the brown bin. I thought that was stupid. I considered it logical to put green waste into a green bin, and my logic had been determined to prevail over my obedience to the garbage bin guru's instructions. Must have been pushed a bit too hard at work. "Could be stress!" I thought as I heard Griff whisper calming thoughts into my ear. If only I had taken one deep breath and reread the notice written in huge letters on the side of the brown bin. This now yelled at me, GARDEN CLIPPINGS ONLY.

Disobey at your peril, I thought morosely while I stood with three bins full of trash all carefully sorted, and all wrong. How could I have done it? Had I spent all of my life carefully putting information into the wrong bins of my mind, sifting and sorting and categorizing and being wrong all the time because I had not read the instructions? If so, what had the instructions been? Where had the instructions been? Who had them and what did they say?

ODD THINGS DO HAPPEN

I am not the only person in the world to experience the odd things that sit me back on my heels like those trash bins. When I took a tram into the city of Melbourne to take my favorite leather boots for repair, I was not looking for tales. Mr. Evans started his business in 1956 in a tiny arcade tucked off to the side of Royal Arcade that has a star-rating for its history. Opened in 1870, it is the oldest surviving arcade in Australia. In the Italianate style, it was designed by Mr. Charles Webb, an architect from Surrey, England.

I remember visiting Royal Arcade with Merle when I was a child and standing in awe under the ornate glass ceilings awaiting the gonging of the enormous carved mythic figures of Gog and Magog that flank Gaunt's clock, which triggers the arms of those figures to strike the bells each quarter hour. Dozens of tourists into Melbourne town still gather with cameras at the ready to take pleasure in this event in the arcade that originally ended with an entrance to a Turkish bath.

I wandered through the Royal Arcade and turned the corner into the Evans Repair Shop. It had not been there as long as Gog and Magog but surely had been there a very long time. Up until recently he, Evan Skliros, had sat presiding over all comings and goings in the business that he had founded more than sixty years before. The business with my boots done, I purchased a tube of violet colored shoe polish and then hovered enjoying conversation with the owner's daughter. "You cannot return this product, you know," she smiled at me. Of course not, I would not consider it.

"Would anybody try?" I laughed. The grin on Mr. Evans's face now moved across and lit up the face of his daughter. "You would not believe what people do," she whispered to me and moved closer, conspiratorial now. "I might," I said. "Tell me." "Some people even try to return shoelaces," she said, her brown eyes widening with affront. "I mean, opened shoelaces! They come in, thrust an opened package at me gesturing their annoyance, completely miffed and saying, 'These are the wrong length!'" We joined Mr. Evans as we all grinned now. One fellow, she went on, had purchased two pairs of laces that came joined together by a narrow paper collar. He came back into the shop some days later with just one of the pairs that he wanted to return for money back, telling her he thought he had purchased one pair and did not want the others—thank you very much. The packet had been opened and the collar torn off! "People can be so odd!" she muttered under her breath. "I told him, 'No sir!' in no uncertain terms. That sure set him back on his heels."

People can be odd. But not me, surely?

THE FACE OF THE MILKMAN

Evan Skliros of Evan's Repair Shop was Greek, as was his family before him. Although my great grandfather Antonio Pavarno Capuano had probably set sail for Australia from the Greek island of Corfu, he was by no means Greek. At least I knew that, but I was beginning to feel as though I had unveiled a family mystery or inadvertently opened a cupboard from which a skeleton had slipped out. Perhaps I had just discovered that the local milkman was my father. I could not push that awkward skeleton back in. The cupboard would not close.

When I was a little girl wearing my dark hair in long plaits tied with ribbons, the milkman came with his horse and cart clip-clopping down our street in the gray of early morning, carrying a load of rattling and clanking milk cans that glinted in the morning half-light. The weary horse would stop at each house while the milkman ran to our back doors to ladle milk orders into cans that had been left outside. But I cannot remember his face. Now I am beginning to wonder if I look at all like him? Perhaps from the side? Trouble is that I never did see him, I was busy sleeping at the time he came down our street with his beautiful clip-clopping horse and clanking milk cans.

The dairy that serviced 45b was at the top of our street, and from time to time I would run up and marvel at the beautiful patient horses awaiting their morning's journey. The trail of manure that followed the milkman and his horse and cart along the suburban streets was scooped up by avid garden-ers, with not a skerrick wasted. "Waste not, want not" was the mantra, right down to manure. But no matter how hard-work-ing our milkman, he cannot have been my father, as it was my mother Annie Merle Capuano Pavarno who carried the Italian name, not Willis.

WORLD WAR I AND ITS ENTRAILS

I have tried to imagine what life could have been like for an eight-year-old girl whose mother had died, leaving her alone at home with a bereaved fifty-two-year-old father and no sib-lings in the house. It was post World War I, and in Australia at that time neither public nor government reaction to Italian immigrants was kind, or even slightly sympathetic. People who were deemed to be "of enemy origin" were progressively more and more tightly controlled by the government. It was the year 1921, and the Australian citizenship was not estab-lished until The Nationality and Citizenship Act of 1948, twenty-seven years later, and did not finally come into effect until 26 January 1949.

During the devastating years of World War I, Australians were still classified as British subjects, while although *living* in Australia, non-British subjects were called "aliens." "People of enemy origin" was the term used to refer to three groups of people in Australia at that time: 1. Aliens from countries at war with Britain. 2. Naturalized British subjects originally from those countries, and 3. British subjects with ancestors from those countries. Parliamentarians warned the citizenry that aliens already living in Australia were likely to take the jobs of Australian soldiers. Public antagonism toward southern and eastern Europeans in Australia was rife by the second half of the war, and they were treated with suspicion. Returned soldiers even went so far as to support riots against Italians, who became known as "the olive peril." By 1917 it was stated publicly that "feeling against enemy aliens is growing." Who should be authorized to decide which people of enemy origin were trustworthy and which were not? Who could carry such a daunting responsibility?

Into the bloody confusion and turmoil just prior to World War I, my mother, Anne Merle Capuano Pavarno was born on Monday, January 6, in the year 1913. People considered to be of enemy origin remained in the minority, and only under certain circumstances were they permitted to become British subjects in Australia through the process of naturalization.

In April of the year 1921, following the carnage and destruction of World War I and its congealing aftermath, Anne Merle's mother died, leaving her to process her unspeakable grief alone, buried in sadness and ostracized socially at school where the abomination of the white-Australia policy still tainted the backwash from that war. Willis told me that Merle was beaten up every day at school just for having the Italian name Capuano.

Merle never spoke of it, but trouble was in her lap. Where could she turn for comfort or reassurance? From the little I heard from her it was not in the arms of her father, Francis

Capuano Pavarno, nor in the arms of her stepmother, Isabella McGregor Murchie Capuano Pavarno. Who would be her helpmeet?

While many parliamentarians were concerned about how to maintain the vital policy of a "white Australia" without offending Britain, how did my step-grandmother from Scotland find her way into this mix? What had caused her to leave Scotland? When and where did Francis Capuano and Isabella McGregor Murchie meet? Was it before or after the death of Merle's mother?

One way or another, by 13 October 1923 Isabella McGregor Murchie had married Francis Capuano Pavarno.

ANTONIO CAPUANO

1816 — 1913

Antonio Capuano Pavarno, my great grandfather. He was the first Capuano-Pavarno in Australia. He jumped ship and stayed until his death sixty years later. What of his progeny? They were there by virtue of birth, but where did they fit into the scheme of Australian policies post World War I?

LURKING AWAY

Behind the doors of the blue-painted kitchen cupboards of 45b there lurked evidence of our Italian heritage, should anyone care to take a look. If you took a peek you could see all the food laid out in orderly Mediterranean rows. If you happened to wander past the cupboard on the way to the back door, an unexpected and gentle aroma of olive oil and sardines assailed you—a mysterious and distinctly un-Australian odor in those days. But despite the Mediterranean food—the sardines, odd cheeses, and olive oil—Merle never did speak of Italy or appear to long to know the history of her Italian heritage. She remained silently a Capuano, her known history clasped tightly to her bosom until it all came to a screeching halt when she applied for the first passport of her life.

According to records, Merle's grandfather Antonio Capuano Pavarno died in 1915. In those first two years of Merle's life, did she ever meet this tall Italian gentleman who sat staring at the camera, stoically buried behind a bushy beard? Did he hold her, cuddle her, play with her, read to her, or talk to her? I do not remember that he was ever mentioned in my presence. Even the most loquacious of my relatives gave me little information.

I began to feel as though I was flapping around at the end of a long, loose string as I battled with my frustration and confusion over my own DNA results. Through my head there ran again and again the 1927 song written at the height of the popularity of the Prince of Wales: Edward VIII, King of the United Kingdom of Great Britain and Ireland and the Dominions of the British Empire, and Emperor of India. "I've danced with a man, who's danced with a girl, who's danced with the Prince of Wales." The astronaut Buzz Aldrin spoke proudly of his connection to Orville Wright through his father Edwin Eugene Aldrin, who was an aviator and officer, saying, "My father was an engineer and an aviation pioneer, and a friend of Charles Lindbergh and Orville Wright." I, too, wanted to be able to point to the connection with the Italians in my paper bag of life. I, too, found myself right down at the end of a line; close, but not directly attached, to *those Italians*. I could not touch them and I was now not sure if they were reaching out to me in this paper bag of life we shared.

On the only occasion when I had raised the courage to ask Merle for information about her father, Francis Capuano Pavarno, who had died while she was pregnant with me, she had slammed the door shut forever on that conversation. What had happened to her, I wondered, as the years of my adult life brought me into a broader understanding of the complex and complicated possibilities of human behavior?

Merle was so closed up, so closed off, so disconnected, despite dressing well and being able to function civilly in company. When I had moved into adult life I approached Willis once with, "Have you ever thought it could be possible that Merle was sexually abused by her father in the years they were alone and before Isabella entered their home?" I was feeling very tentative about even raising the subject, unsure if he would even know what I was talking about as neither sexual behavior nor sexual misbehavior had ever been discussed in our family. He stood very still with his head down for a while, breathing unhappiness. Then, turning his body half toward me, his face distraught, he shocked me with, "I have thought of that myself." And he walked away. And I walked away. We never spoke of it again. What lurked there unspoken?

No wonder she never held my hand as we crossed a busy city street. No wonder she never walked to the bus station with me early in the morning, or waited with me to be sure I was safely on the bus on my way to school. No wonder she never came to parent-teacher meetings and left me as the only child with no parent present. No wonder she hand stitched a plainly awful speech-night dress for me instead of taking me to shop for a special outfit as all the other mothers had done. It was the cheapest she could offer, not the best. And now no wonder I enjoy indulging myself with lovely clothes, filling the gap as I go, entertaining myself daily with my favorite form of play. Nothing boring, thank you. No beige for me, thank you. There are Italians in my paper bag!

The Italians in Merle's paper bag of life had all been tied up, tied down, locked up, and locked in somewhere deep inside where neither Merle nor anyone else in that big scary outside world could ever know about them. There was shame there. There had been enough hurt, and she was not about to be hurt again. She lived her life one fearful step at a time, without much comment about Italians.

ECLECTIC RELLIES

The presence of the many Italians living in Australia from the landings of Captain Cook through to the Eureka Stockade has been described as both eclectic and accidental. Hence it was, that I felt free to conclude that my great-grandfather Antonio's arrival on Australian shores could rightly be considered both eclectic and accidental. Now I have decided that since "eclectic" sounds resoundingly more interesting than "accidental," I shall be considering my rellies as *eclectic* from now on. "Deriving ideas, style, or taste from a broad and diverse range of sources," states my dictionary about eclectic. That will do me.

One imaginative branch of this eclectic family of mine even went so far as to change their name from Capuano to Capp by Deed Poll because of the anti-Italian sentiment in Australia following Mussolini's alliance with Germany during World War II.

Mussolini was not finally overthrown until July 1943; yet despite Mussolini, Australia—with its growing infrastructure requirements and lack of unskilled labor—found itself in great need of an enlarged population. In consequence of this pressing need, by 1947 the number of Italian immigrants in Australia had grown to 289,476. The rich legacy of Italian immigration has brought hundreds of thousands of people of Italian descent to become actively integrated into Australian society, which leaves me with no reason to feel different. As one of this vast diaspora, I rather liked the exotic nature of such a heritage, despite the sad fact that it carried with it a dark underbelly.

ALL THAT GLITTERS

Since the year 1788, millions of people have made the long journey across the oceans to Australia seeking fortune and freedom, filled with the hope of all new possibilities, their fancies multiplying as they sailed. Those journeys during the nineteenth century were long and dangerous, with the sailing ships taking from two to four months. Severe storms were common in the Southern Ocean and food and hygiene aboard ship were poor.

By the year 1823 there was a stirring in the ranks in Australia when traces of gold were discovered near Bathurst by a Mr. James McBrien. The authorities did make a brave attempt to hush up discoveries such as his, afraid that all convicts, soldiers, and public servants would stop work and set off to hunt for their fortune. When the Reverend W. B. Clarke found a nugget near Cox's River in the Blue Mountains of New South Wales in 1841, he was admonished by Governor Gipps to, "Put it away, Mr. Clarke, or we shall all have our throats cut!" Cut throats or no, the dramatic publication of a find near Bathurst by Edward Hargraves in 1851 led to more than one thousand men looking for gold within one month. Two percent of the population of the British Isles emigrated to New

South Wales during the 1850s, as well as Europeans, North Americans, and Chinese.

Into this roiling, boiling phalanx of miners—with their rockers and gold pans, sluice boxes and shovels, tents and billy cans, picks and buckets, wheelbarrows and rope—walked the Italian Antonio Capuano Pavarno, far from the land of his birth and ready to give it a go in this land of opportunity. The year was 1854. From the port of Geelong, he had walked first to Spring Mount and then on to Jim Crow, later to be renamed Daylesford. This was a distance of about one hundred kilometers, or sixty-two miles. Approximately six thousand diggers were arriving each week, seeking their fortune.

The discovery of gold dramatically boosted Australia's development—Melbourne earning the nickname "Marvelous Melbourne" and drawing comparisons to Paris and London due to the influx of wealth and migrants. The economic and cultural impact of this mass migration shaped the future of Victoria. Within ten years of the gold rushes to Bathurst, Ballarat, and Bendigo, Australia's population trebled to more than one million people. Even today, Victoria remains a world-renowned gold province with a history closely linked to gold mining.

One government inspector spoke of coming upon what appeared to be a sea of white as the diggers lay spread-eagled in their moleskins, clinging to the earth side by side for as far as the eye could see. It is said that the early prospectors were lying thus attempting to hold on to their promise-filled claims with every inch of their bodies. Their white moleskin trousers were made of hard-wearing cotton first used by farmers and hunters who needed clothing that was comfortable, warm, durable, and wind resistant. It was said to feel as soft as a mole. Hence, the name moleskin.

RING THE BELLS

Far away over the sea in Scotland, the trauma of the Highland Clearances and competition for land, jobs, and housing had caused thousands of Scots to leave and set sail for the new world from the mid-to-late eighteenth century–on. The Clearances were the forced eviction of many farmer inhabitants of the Highlands and western islands of Scotland that cleared the lands of people primarily to allow for the introduction of sheep pastoralism. As families were dispossessed of their land, to a large extent they were also dispossessed of their culture. Many Highlanders were forced into exile. The Clearances were known to the Gaelic-speaking Highlanders as the *Bliadhna nan Caorach*, (Year of the Sheep).

On 27 May 1839, one Francis Bell of Lochmaben, County of Dumfries in Scotland, made application to become an "Emigrant Laborer for a Free Passage to Australia" from Scotland. At the time of the application his occupation was as a domestic servant at Bridgemoor, Lochmaben. He was twenty-four years old, while his wife, Janet, was only twenty and had already birthed two daughters, two-year-old Agnes, and three-month-old Elizabeth.

Times were hard for many in Scotland, and Francis was

possibly seeking a better life for his young family. Their ship, the *Lady Lilford*, sailed from Liverpool on Tuesday, 18 June 1839 under the care of a Captain James Kermath and arrived at Port Adelaide on Friday, 27 September 1839 with 203 passengers on board. Of the intrepid travelers, Francis and Janet Bell and their two daughters, Elizabeth and Agnes, were to become my forebears. Francis gained employment as a farm laborer in the Adelaide district. There they resided until he upped and ran, disappearing from Adelaide in about 1850, leaving his young wife, Janet, with six children ranging in age from three to thirteen years old. It is remarkable that according to the laws of the land at the time, Janet was unable to remarry until husband Francis had been missing for twenty years. She was abandoned and neglected, left to care for their six children alone. And yet the law was set up so that she was made to look to some as though her desperate plight was her own fault.

But nobody thought to leave me a note or letter to explain, and I am left wondering how this young Scottish lass, mother of six, ever survived so much grief and hardship while living far from the land of her birth.

WEDDING BELLS

I read that by the time she was nineteen, Janet's Bell's eldest daughter Agnes was working near the busy goldfields of Creswick in Victoria. It was there that she became acquainted with a gentleman of Italian origin who was thirty-eight years old and searching for gold in the creeks and shallow diggings around Creswick. His name was Antonio Pavarno Capuano, and by then he had been resident in Australia for approximately six years. Thus, it came about that seventeen years after arriving in Australia as a two-year-old, Agnes Little Bell married Antonio Pavarno Capuano on Saturday, 28 June 1856. How did they become acquainted? Did she love him? Did he love her? I know not how it was that they met nor whether theirs was a love shared, but one way or another, their union was the beginning of the Capuano family in Australia. They are my Italian family. They are the Italians in my paper bag.

But where is the evidence of Antonio in my DNA now? There is certain evidence of Scottish DNA, 28 percent, *they* tell me, thus I know that Agnes's genes took a grip. But what has happened to Antonio's DNA? I had always thought that I was bone of their bone, flesh of their flesh—but now my birthday-present-DNA result tells me, no. Nada. Definitely not. Nothing. Zero. Nix. Nic. Niets. Nichts. Nimic. Or in Italian, niente.

Scottish? Yes. Italian? No. English? Yes. Italian? No. Irish? Yes. Italian? No. French? Yes. What's this? *French?*

No matter which way I look at it, I come up with the same response. "Nothing at all to be seen here," *they* say about my Italian heritage, leaving me feeling as flummoxed and daunted as Merle must have done when she was told, "No. You do not exist!"

AUSTRALIAN ABORIGINAL MYTHOLOGY

We have *bunyips* in Australia in the Aboriginal Dreaming stories about the world and its creation. Bunyips are mythical creatures that are said in these tales to lurk around waterholes, swamps, *billabongs*, and creeks. They have been described as having "shining, baleful eyes and a bellowing voice." Sometimes they are called *yowies,* which are spirits that roam over the earth at night. There even exists a swamp in the valley of the New South Wales Highlands that is home to the rare giant dragonfly, which is part of an ancient group of insect fliers common during the age of the dinosaurs. Bunyips are supposed to lurk in the depths of this swamp. Bill Wanna in his book, *Australian Folklore,* informs me that "bunyips are said to devour humans, coming up on them in silence and when least expected."

As I ponder this, I think there is a fair chance that it could have been a bunyip or a yowie that crept out of the bog to steal the Italians in my paper bag when I was not looking.

CHINESE WHISPERS

The stories of Antonio Capuano Pavarno that have been passed down from earlier generations have led me to believe that this, my first Italian ancestor in Australia, came from either Corfu or Corsica with his brother Michael, who was captain of the ship that sailed to Australia to the port of Geelong, arriving in about 1852. There Antonio jumped ship and headed for the gold diggings of Victoria while his brother Michael continued to sail on for the New World of the United States of America.

Antonio and Michael were two of a family of six children. Their mother is shown as Nunciato Amusto and their father as Spiro Capuano, but sometimes as Spiro Pavarno, and sometimes even as Johannes Capuano. It makes me wish to stand on my head in an effort to perceive what was going on here. There was early confusion with the Italians in my paper bag. The Capuano-Pavarno family had migrated from the Italian port of Barletta on the Adriatic coast of Italy in the year 1830, to live on the Greek island of Corfu, less than fifty miles from mainland Italy and a convenient stopover port for all ships on their way to Italy. Corfu was also known as Corcyra, which sounds similar to Corsica, and may explain the confusion as to the place Antonio departed from on his journey to Australia. After living for some time in the United States, Antonio's brother Michael apparently returned to Corfu, where he lived with his family until his death in 1904. He is buried in Corfu.

By the 1850s and 60s, all new arrivals in Australia were labeled as "New Australians," with Italians forming the largest non-English-speaking group. Pejorative names specific to Italians at that time were "dago" and "eyetie." They were also called wogs or wops. All these names were insulting, tarring the recipients with the intended ethnic slur. They were offensive terms intended to offend. They were contemptuous and disparaging, and used disrespectfully.

EARTH WANDERERS

At the time of Antonio's travel to Australia the journey was a long and dangerous two-to-four months via sailing ship, with storms common in the Southern Ocean. His brother Michael would have needed a good working knowledge of the position of the stars in the night sky as well as the use of various navigational tools as he made passage through some of the world's most treacherous waters.

Was gold the only incentive for Antonio's journey? Alluvial gold was discovered in Wombat Flat, Bathurst, in 1851 by an Irish immigrant, John Egan. By 1859 there were approximately 3,400 diggers on the local diggings, so that by 1860 the alluvial gold was exhausted, and it was essential to make a shift to quartz-reef mining. Many Italians migrated to Australia around this time due to poor conditions, rebellions, and overpopulation in Italy, and they congregated in what later became known as Daylesford but was then known as Jim Crow. Jim Crow was first established in the year 1852 as a gold-mining town. Whatever the means of communication across the oceans, Antonio carried with him a fair-sized bundle of determination and courage as he sailed toward Australia, perhaps dreaming of gold.

By the time Anne Merle Capuano Pavarno Richards was living through the 1950s and 60s, all new arrivals in Australia were labeled "new Australians," with Italians forming the largest non-English-speaking group. These immigrants suffered a litany of pejorative names specific to Italians. What of Merle? Did she suffer such indignities, or worse? She never spoke of it.

FLAT OUT LIKE A LIZARD
DRINKING WATER

I have taken to feeling deflated. Not popped like the party balloon at the end of celebrations—but flat, lifeless, and lacking in energy—a little sad and also a little astonished at my response to all this lack of connection to what I had thought were my Italian roots. Up until the shock of the DNA results, I had no idea how much my Italian mob held me enthralled. They had been as a light musical air pulsing along in the background of my life, a flute solo here, the high note of a piccolo there, with the occasional wonder of Yo-Yo Ma's cello music thrown in to sweeten up the pasta sauce.

But nothing? Why has this disturbed me so, I ask myself. Why am I saddened by my lack of the Italian mob's blood racing, or even loitering, through my veins? Had I dared to be arrogant about the slightly exotic nature of this lineage? With stories of the manner in which the "eyeties" were treated in Australia, anything exotic in my life owes its all to my imagination. It seems to be more about the fragrance of that imaginary pasta sauce simmering in the kitchen of 45b. But mother Merle was not an Italian mama by any means of anyone's imagination, nor was she a *nona*, being neither particularly motherly nor particularly grandmotherly. Although I have to say that she did not have much chance to interact with Luke

Benjamin and Toby John, and she met Nathan David only once when he was a tiny babe. So, what is it that I am missing as I look at the sad little map of Italy the DNA-gurus emailed to me, with its ruinous dotted lines drawn hither and yon—and where, under the enticing heading Northern Italy, it yells at me: *"No connection!"* Then, underneath Sicily, yells some more, *"No connection!"* And again, underneath Southern Italy, yells, *"No connection!"* Calabria, Campania, Basilicata, Campania and Molise, Lazio and Campania, Puglia, Salerno, Umbria, Abruzzo, and Lazio, NO CONNECTION!

I am cut off from my moorings like that deflated balloon dragging sadly along the ground, untethered, unwanted, and not useful for anything—at least not useful for anything Italian. I have to get over this. What is it that I don't know about my life, my family, and my Italian heritage? What I thought I knew is not sticking to me these days. What I thought was my life is not my life. What else do I not know about my life? Did any of the people I met along the tracks—as I wandered through hills and dales, beside frantic freeways and forgotten side roads, in and out of cities and countries all over the world—have a clue for me that I missed, simply because I did not think to ask? What I thought I knew to be true I held lightly. That is, until some devious expert decided to take it right out of my hands, my life, my blood, my connection, and my heritage. Where did they put it? Did they toss it to one side like so much flotsam? Or did they creep into the broom cupboard at night and dump it in the wastepaper basket simply to spite me or because they were bored and looking for fun? Did they consign the Italians in my paper bag to oblivion deliberately?

The DNA kit had requested politely, "Before you spit, activate your kit." I did.

Then further, printed in red ink and highlighted with an exclamation point, they demanded, "Do NOT eat, drink, smoke, or chew gum for 30 MINUTES before giving your saliva sample." I did not dare.

INTENTIONAL

For a few years I worked with a gentleman who would stare at me from time to time until I became uncomfortably aware of him. Once I looked up, he would let out a short sigh before saying in a rather arrogantly sanitized voice, "You are very intentional, Jillian. Very intentional." It was hard for me to say if his was a sigh of frustration or of disbelief. "Oh?" I would shrug, unsure of his meaning and awaiting an explanation. But in all the years we worked together he never did explain what he was thinking about me, or why. Intentional? I had never been closely associated with anyone who had used that term about me, or about anyone else. Was it a compliment? A criticism? He did not say, or even infer. It was a blunt statement of fact on his part that left me unsure as to whether he wanted me to question him further or interpret his meaning for myself. He offered no lead into his statement, just the stare and the sanitized voice.

Having read once about an artist who stated that the heart

channels the hand, it could follow that the heart channels the words we say, or do not say. I observe that language as a tool carries with it power enough to create or to destroy, to build up or to put down—even to give or take life itself. A few words fitly spoken can be life-changing. His few words repeated from time to time were not life-changing, but they were puzzling. They are puzzling still.

The very few words that came riding in on my computer telling me of my lack of Italian DNA have in their own small way been life-changing for me. They have definitely been head-changing and are working their way up to being paradigm-changing. Now I will have the need to be intentionally intentional about my thinking, and particularly regarding my heritage.

ADROIT

In the trove of detritus from Willis's life I found a tired envelope on which was written by hand: References of Character. Inside this tatty remnant lay a reference written in 1959 by Willis's RAAF Commanding Officer. It is complimentary in every way, but the closing sentence is my favorite. "I have no hesitation in recommending him for any executive position which calls for efficiency, adroitness, loyalty and sobriety." I smiled at the *sobriety*, having recently discovered from a cousin that, during the many years I spent living in the United States, Willis would visit her for family celebrations and would always ask her husband if he happened to have any Scotch in the house. And I had always thought he never touched a drop! But *adroitness*? Now, that set me back on my heels. I could not recall ever having heard it used in everyday speech. Did I inherit the adroitness gene instead of the Italian one? Is adroitness akin to *intentional*, or even *international*? Could I practice being *adroit*? Was it a character trait, an inherited gene, or a quirk? Would I want it if I could find out what it was? "Jillian is adroit." How would that sound?

When Willis was a young man newly arrived in Melbourne town from life on the farm at St. James, he would have been looking for employment. He never did tell me where he went when he got off the train from St. James. Perhaps there was a cousin or some other farm escapee who took him in while he found his feet. Ancient references in the tatty envelope tell me that in April 1930, Willis was resident at 7 Denbigh Road, Armadale, Victoria. With whom did he live or share accommodation? In that reference he is referred for his "sobriety, industry, and attention to duty." By May of the same year, over the signature of a member of the Parliament in Victoria whose name I cannot decipher, Willis is said to be, "a very fine type of young man, of temperate habits and heart." I do like the temperate heart bit but still think adroit is more fun and continue to remain unsure about intentional. By March 1937, Willis was working for O. Gilpin Ltd., and in their reference is said to be "an honest and willing worker, punctual in attendance and thoroughly reliable." By April 1938, Willis was working with Hatchers Laundry Pty. Ltd, and the manager there said of him that he was "trustworthy and efficient." After all that, I still prefer adroitness. I think I will take that on as part of my DNA, at least until I understand what it is.

Willis (left), straight off the farm in the Depression, cleaning the reservoir at Reservoir. Any work was good work in those days. Perhaps it was at the reservoir in Reservoir that he learned to be adroit. Were there Italians, adroit or other, working alongside him in that reservoir in Reservoir?

CHECKING, CHECKING

I have met many purposeful folk in my life, yet I did not think to ask a one of them about any possible Italian connection.

COLIN

I looked up at four-star General Colin Luther Powell, former United States Secretary of State, when I met him—and I saw a remarkably fine man. A politician and diplomat, he stood calm and focused, with shoulders broad enough to carry weighty responsibilities. His long list of military awards included two Purple Hearts.

I knew him to have been born in the South Bronx of Jamaican immigrant parents, both of whom were of African and Scottish ancestry. Had he ever been accused of being a "birther"? How had he managed to keep his equanimity? Had he needed to fight to retain his sense of self in the face of adversity from those who believed and continue to believe that to be white and male was the thing to be? Guarding the history of his life and incredible achievements must have taken him into a fight or two of huge proportions.

But I did not think to ask him about any possible Italian connection. Nor did I think to ask him if he had sent a drop or two of his gentlemanly spittle to the DNA-masters who held the right to tell you who you are, and why you can never question their word, for they know that they are the arbiters of all things to do with blood and its secrets. And I did not think to ask General Powell about my Italian heritage either. It was not a question in my mind then. The Italian bit had always been there, and I had never thought to question it. It was just what it was, and where it was. There.

Even as he stood with his hand around my waist.

General Powell has stated that trust, accepting failure, and remaining optimistic are keys to his understanding of successful leadership. "One team, one fight," he has said. He has also said that he tries to take a failure as a beginning, because "You have learned something about yourself." I, too, have learned something about myself, even though it has no relationship to that which I expected to learn. In his book, *My American Journey*, General Powell speaks of his love for the United States of America and its people. "We are a fractious nation, always searching, always dissatisfied, yet always hopeful. We have an infinite capacity to rejuvenate ourselves." And I reflect that these capacities are those of the millions of people who wander this earth seeking a place to call home, adapting and adopting, again and again—and again.

When I looked once more at that photo of the two of us standing close beside each other at the end of our conversation, I notice that Secretary of State, Chairman of the Joint Chiefs of Staff, National Security Advisor, Commander of the Armed Forces, four-star General Colin Luther Powell has his arm firmly around my waist. I rushed to the telephone and called elder son Luke Benjamin urgently. "Should I crop this?" "No way, Ma," he laughed, "leave it right where it is."

With Secretary of State, Chairman of the Joint Chiefs of Staff, National Security Advisor, Commander of US Army Forces, four-star General Colin Luther Powell.

SURVIVING AUSTRALIA

Antonio Capuano Pavarno worked as a miner in Petticoat Gully, Creswick, as well as in Back Creek and Cabbage Tree, and was unfortunate enough to have been employed at the New Australasian Mine in 1882, when Australia's greatest belowground gold-mining disaster occurred. It was there that twenty-nine miners were trapped underground as floodwaters poured in from the parallel-sunk No.1 mineshaft. The trapped men scrawled last notes to their loved ones on billycans (their light weight cooking pots) before they drowned. Some of these billycans are displayed at the Creswick Museum. It is hard to think of it. Those drowned miners left eighteen widows and seventy-five dependent children.

Antonio was one of the only five miners who survived, although his arms and legs were broken, leaving him "incapacitated from work for some time." Antonio later described himself as "crippled ever since." Despite the severity of his injuries he lived to the great age of ninety-seven, dying at Red Gully, Creswick, on 12 June 1915, leaving a widow, four sons, and two daughters.

Antonio had put a lot of trust in his brother Michael to carry him safely across the oceans to the shores of Australia, which indicates that both were courageous risk-takers. Did what Antonio found in Australia have any relationship to what he had expected to find? Was he surprised, pleased, daunted, overwhelmed, afraid, or lonely? Was he, too, adroit—like

Willis? Was he a fair man, a just man, or a fine man? Or was he escaping a failed marriage when he sailed from Corfu for far-off Australian shores? Did he leave children behind? A marriage? Was he curious, determined, prevaricating, or simply seeking his fortune?

In Antonio's memoir from 1900 he tells the tale of tramping from Jump Up to Creswick, humping his gold-washing cradle and tub on his back, and being accompanied by a large dog. He speaks of meeting "another party" who was also accompanied by a dog as his protector. The two dogs' rough and tumble at their meeting led to fisticuffs on the part of Antonio and the "other party." Antonio was further annoyed by his new acquaintance when he was asked repeatedly which country he was from. "The population at the time," he said, "was a most cosmopolitan one." That would have to have been an understatement. As the conversation moved on, he was to discover to his surprise that the inquirer and he had been known to each other in Italy, and he (Antonio) had been recognized.

Ultimately Antonio found gold to the value of 190 Australian pounds, the current value of which would be approximately $16,000 AUD. This small fortune represented all that Antonio had in his new Australian home. But greed got the better of his working companion, and as has been the wont of man from time to time, his companion ran off one dark night with Antonio's gold and other goodies—never to be found again, leaving Antonio to start over. As am I. Again and again, and again.

HOTEL WINDSOR

There were times in my youth when Merle would take me into the city of Melbourne on the tram to visit with an aunt who was resident in the Hotel Windsor. Built at the height of Victoria's gold rush and at the time of early rural prosperity, the Windsor was considered a magnificent dream when it was constructed by shipping magnate George Nipper. It is still considered to be Australia's most loved hotel, and predates the Savoy in London, the Plaza and the Waldorf Astoria in New York, and Raffles in Singapore. Knowing nothing of its history and supposed splendor, I grew up thinking it quite normal for anyone's aunt to be resident in the Windsor and presumed for many years that when I was an aunt I, too, would move in to occupy my very own suite where my relatives would visit me as I sat gracious and welcoming in the comfort of one who is well-looked-after.

Somewhere along the way on one of these trips, Merle told me very quietly that the aunt living so comfortably in the Windsor belonged to "the other side of the family"—*the other side* being the ones whose forebear had run off in the night with Antonio's gold and other goodies, and hence the riches that were now on display. I said nothing but scoffed internally, thinking that perhaps this was all talk from a jealous relative. Who had ever heard of a family member running off with gold in the nighttime? It sounded more than far-fetched to my young ears.

Merle owned one elegant gold bar that she occasionally pinned to her lapel and into which was set a magnificent opal. She told me that the aunt who was resident in the Windsor had given this to her as a token of her regret at the family tale. I was pleased to be gifted this pin when I was an adult and wore it with pride until the day that I took it from my dress in the changing room of the ladies' department of the Myer department store. I placed it carefully on a tiny shelf, tried on my new clothes and walked off to the counter to make my purchase. It took me not more than two minutes to remember that I had left the precious brooch behind. By the time I high-tailed it back to the changing room three minutes later, the brooch was gone.

ADOPTION

"I have had much hardship, but am still able to move about in my eighty-ninth year, having lived in the country of my adoption for nearly sixty years." So wrote Antonio in his memoir. On 12 June 1915, Antonio Capuano Pavarno died at Red Gully, Creswick. His obituary claims him to have been "the oldest resident of Creswick." He was described as "one of the sturdy pioneers, of robust good health, and was able to get around until the final summons came." I do love the get-around bit. One way or another he did get around: from Italy to the Greek island of Corfu, and thence to the goldfields of Victoria, where he would ultimately join in the Eureka Stockade Uprising of 3 December 1854. This was a rebellion by the gold prospectors against the exorbitant prospect-license fees and the brutal police procedures for collecting those fees.

Gold prospectors were known by the term "diggers" and there were reported to have been 150 diggers holed up within the hastily built stockade where the fierce battle between the diggers and the police lasted a brief fifteen minutes. The fury of the diggers at their longstanding grievances had finally boiled over, and they were determined to defend their rights against what they saw as unfair taxation by the government. This Eureka uprising is considered to be the beginning of democracy in Australia, but in that brutally short battle twenty-two diggers and five troopers were killed. Ultimately, all the diggers' desperate demands were met, including the abolition of the License and Gold Commission.

And Antonio was right there in the midst of the turmoil. And he was Italian. And he is my great-grandfather.

The term, digger, also became the nickname for Australian soldiers fighting overseas and comes from the fact that in World War I, many of these soldiers had literally been diggers in the goldfields just prior to the war.

Australia continues to be one of the world's top producers of gold.

And again I ponder which parts of my Italian heritage have leeched away, and where did they go? Have they bolted off over the fence and far away into the nether parts of the universe, or flown off into universes that we do not yet know?

FEATHERING MY NEST

And then there was Phil.

It happened that one bright California day. I found myself propped against an enormous plate glass window and scanning the campus for what promised to be an intriguing guest by the name of Chief Phil Stevens, a Newport Beach engineer who had been named Special Chief of the Great Sioux nation—the title of *Itancankel*, or Special Chief, having been bestowed upon him by the chief of the Oglala tribe, Red Cloud.

I was pleasuring in the warmth of the sun, which was peeping over the neatly trimmed hedge that lined the pathway in front of me, when my eye was caught by what I thought at first was a bird in flight. But as I stood puzzling away, I observed that this particular Californian bird was neither hop, hop, hopping or bop, bop bopping along—and was generally behaving nothing at all like the pair of blue jays that inhabited the backyard of my Orange County home. I was about to glance away from the bright plumage that had caught my eye when I realized what was taking its own flight path toward me. I grasped at the air in front of me for support as I doubled over in laughter, for turning the corner at the end of the hedge and grinning mischievously at my mirth, came Phil. The bob, bob, bobbing had been the tips of the feathers of the gorgeous war bonnet of the Sioux plains people as he walked toward me along the pathway, hidden by the neatly trimmed hedge. It took one full minute for me to come to my senses, greet Phil, and move quickly on to covet not only his elaborate and spectacular war bonnet but the rest of his outfit as well. I remain miffed at myself that I did not think to ask for it, or at least a very good copy. It was a splendid statement of celebration, and I know it would have suited me well. All that buckskin and fringing and feathers and belts and pouches sure suited *him* well. His face was suffused with beaming joy, and I do think he must have exalted in gearing up for any parade he could find. I would have given up any claim to Italian heritage at that moment in exchange for his gorgeous regalia.

Unsympathetic folk told me later that Phil was a bit of a hustler, while others more sympathetic told me that he was a good man who, amongst many other things, had led an entourage through the Bear Butte State Park and the Mount Rushmore Memorial long before The Donald ever thought of it. Phil is proud to be three-sixteenths Sioux and claims to be the great-grandson of the warrior chief Standing Bear.

I was so mesmerized by Phil and his regalia that, once again, I was left frustrated with myself, knowing that I needed to be quicker. I could and should have asked him if he had ever sent a jot or tittle of his spittle off to the DNA-masters of the universe who could give or take one's sense of self with a few short and masterly sentences? I was so enamored of Phil's regalia that I did not think to ask. I knew that I was the great-granddaughter of an Italian who had crossed the vast oceans from Corfu to Australia in the 1800s, and because of this fact I had never thought to question that I had Italian blood coursing through my veins. There was no question as far as I knew. Up until then.

I was a girl of Italian heritage. I was with a man of Sioux heritage. I wish I had thought to ask Phil how he was so certain of his heritage. If he could use his three-sixteenths claim to Sioux heritage and become the first war chief of the Great Sioux Nation in more than a century—surely, we were not that different, Phil and I. I had two-sixteenths Italian after all. Or so I had thought up until DNA-heaven intervened. What, if any, Italian could I claim now? The mystery remained. Where were those Italians hiding?

With Special Chief Phil Stevens of the Great Sioux Nation.

DECIPHERING

Deoxyribonucleic Acid is the chemical name for the molecule that carries the genetic instructions for all living things. "DNA rearranges itself when egg meets sperm," I read. What they omitted to tell me is that information about your DNA can rearrange your core belief about your roots, your ancestry, and your simply comfortable sense of belonging.

In the year 1953, the American biologist James Watson and English physicist Francis Crick reached their groundbreaking conclusion that the DNA molecule exists in the form of a three-dimensional double helix. Using cardboard cutouts to represent the individual components of the four bases and other nucleotide subunits, Watson and Crick shifted molecules around on their desktops as though putting together a puzzle. Now we know a great deal about genetic structure, and great strides continue to be made in understanding the human genome and the importance of DNA to life and health.

I read that DNA is the cell's hereditary material containing instruction for development, growth, and reproduction, and that deoxyribonucleic acid is a molecule that contains the biological instructions that make each species unique. But by far the best information I read blurted out across the page, "DNA unwinds so it can be copied. At other times in the cell cycle, DNA also unwinds so that its instructions can be used to make proteins and other biological processes." I was beginning to revel in all this scientific information.

For a moment or two I thought I was privy to the best of the explanations. But no! I was beset with an overpowering desire to run from my computer in order to laugh and cry all at the same time when the very best of the hardly digestible material told me that "The complete DNA instruction book, or genome, for a human contains about 3 billion bases and about 20,000 genes on 23 pairs of chromosomes."

"Oh heck!" as Mac would say. What exactly had allowed itself to unwind in my DNA? What had happened to the Italians in my paper bag of life? Had they unwound? Or had they been unwound by virtue of my enquiries? Or had they stopped fussing about any of it and settled down quietly, whispering only to themselves where none of the youngsters like me would ever hear, and where DNA-gurus did not hold sway?

On the back of this scrap Willis wrote, "Half of me left. Taken at St. James when I was about 2 years old. Say 1911. Love, Dad."

What would Willis's DNA have told him?

CONFIDENCE

"Confidence is the feeling you have before you fully understand the situation." I had kept the little business card with this statement printed proudly on its back tucked away in a file for years. It sounded so good. So true. But as I read it again years later, I desired valiantly to make a correction. "Not a feeling!" I cried into the ether. "It is much more likely to be considered a character trait. It is not an emotion; it is a way of being, a personality trait likely to be a cause of emotions or feelings." I underline the word "cause" in my mind as I think on this again. And as I cry in my soup over the results of my no-Italian DNA test I check my pulse and wonder aloud to the walls where I stay locked away to hide from the threat of Covid-19, "Has the no-Italian result hammered away at my confidence about who I am, or has it upended who I am or indeed changed who I am?" Does this alter any character trait of mine?

It is certain that I did not fully understand my DNA situation before, but on the other hand the only new information I have is the DNA itself. Not one other item in the list of items from the family history that I carry in files, or in my memory, or in my heart, has changed.

There sure has been a little riffling of the waters as I have perused the maps of Italy marked up by the DNA-gurus with their cranky pointing negative dots and dashes.

But I am who I am, and Buddy Rogers helped me along the way.

A GIRL NEEDS A BUDDY

Friends invited me to join them in Palm Springs for a celebratory gathering. "Come on, Jillian," they begged, "there will be film stars there! You will have fun."

It pleasured me each time I took the route from Orange County to Las Vegas town or into Palm Springs, or into any town I was privileged to visit in the desert. The colors warmed my spirit. The air felt easy. My favorite Merc purred its way along like a cat edging up to a bowl of cream. My mood lifted. I felt a freedom under the cast-blue canopy of sky. I reveled in the warmth. There was something exciting on offer each time I entered the desert towns.

Among the assembled throng at this evening's adventure, I met a gentleman known by many to be both rich and famous. I noticed that on his immaculate lapel he was wearing a very attractive gold heart. We chatted for a while until I could no longer resist the urge to know the story about the golden heart. "Tell me about the heart," I asked. He frowned down at me in a puzzled kind of way, leaned toward me with a smile, and gently rebuked me as he laid his hand on my shoulder. "Jillian, you mean you don't recognize this heart? This," he said now pointing with pride and tapping the heart reverently and with gentle admonishment, "is the heart that represents the Variety Club."

"Oh," I said, none the wiser but doing my level best to look intelligent. "Tell me about that."

He smiled his pleasure and rolled happily on into the history of the Variety Club. Founded in 1927 by a group of eleven theatre owners and showmen who had heard a babe crying somewhere in their auditorium, the club has become known as a national treasure. After hearing the babe's cries, the group of eleven went searching through the auditorium and came upon a baby girl who was whimpering quietly. Pinned to the clothing of this one-month-old baby girl was a handwritten note making a desperate plea that the child be looked after. Her mother, who had eight other children and a husband out of work, had left her beloved child in the auditorium, hoping that she would be taken up into the arms of the show business people, whom her mother trusted to be good-hearted and generous. The note was signed, "A heartbroken mother."

Despite much searching, the baby girl's parents were never found. The little one ultimately went on to become an inspiration for the international children's charity known as Variety. She was duly named Catherine Variety Sheridan, her middle name for the club and her last name for the theatre where she was found in Pittsburgh, Pennsylvania. This charity, with its roots in the entertainment industry, continues to welcome people from all walks of life to experience the joy of helping a child.

I was so entranced by his story that I moved toward my new friend and whispered, "I would love that heart." I meant this only as an idea, as the whole concept was inspirational.

But he hesitated not, unpinned the gold heart from his lapel and handed it to me.

"Come with us, Jillian," I had been cajoled when I was invited to the Palm Springs "do." "There will be a lot of film stars there, and you will have fun." Thus, it was that one more time in Tinsel Town I had donned my glad rags, fluffed up my hair, and raced off toward the desert in my trusty Merc.

The couple who were my gracious hosts for the weekend spent the rest of that night awed and surprised at the gift of my gold heart. Again and again, they turned as if surprised, expostulating, "Jillian! He gave you his heart. We can't believe it! We can't believe he gave it to you. You are so lucky!" What they did not know was that I had asked for it. That was all.

I had been told once to simply ask, or to ask simply, and I had learned along the way that I would have nothing to lose. I would be no worse off after asking, and if good fortune came my way, I might just find myself with a gold heart on my lapel.

It was a sparkling evening in every way, those gathered were a friendly lot—vivacious and welcoming and ready to chat with an Australian girl so very far from Melbourne town. I sussed them out one by one and in the end determined the best-looking man of the gathering to be Robert Selleck, the father of Tom Selleck of *Magnum P. I.* fame. Tom was a popular TV star at that time and seriously good-looking, but in my humble opinion his father outpaced him at every turn for flat-out good looks.

With Bob and Martha Selleck.

I did enjoy myself, and when toward the end of the dinner I found myself happily seated beside Charles (Buddy) Rogers, the film star and jazz musician who had been married to Mary Pickford for forty-two years, I was pleased. Buddy had a Hollywood Walk of Fame star that had been dedicated at 6135 Hollywood Boulevard in 1960, and a Golden Palm Star dedicated on the Palm Springs Walk of Fame in 1993. Honored in Hollywood for his tireless humanitarian work, Buddy starred in more than forty films, both silent and sound, including the Oscar Award-winning film *Wings*, in which he starred with Clara Bow. Hundreds of pilots were involved in the filming of *Wings*, which would have cost $30 million USD in today's money.

Bob Hope said of him, "He is one of the nicest people I have ever met," and Buddy Rogers was certainly charming company as we sat together chatting away. Up until that moment I was a complete stranger to him, and yet he reflected openly to me on his life and his current feelings about mortality. I found myself drawn into a deeply personal and touching conversation, and was honored to be his companion. He was both reflective and frank, and thoughtful and challenging. I treasured those moments, and he also seemed to treasure them. He turned to face me directly after about thirty minutes, gazing at me for a while, smiling gently. Then he reached out to me with great tenderness, took my chin in his hand, and after turning my face gently one way and another said, "You should be in the movies."

What more could a girl possibly need as an offering from a Hollywood legend?

I reflected on Buddy's deeply personal offering to me as I drove home. In that sanctified moment in time and space we had been as close companions. He trusted me with his questions, not attempting to give answers, but trusting me to reflect back to him that which I had gleaned from life up until then. It was a huge gift of trust. Neither age, nor experience, nor life style, nor connections placed limitations on what was shared. He had allowed me, whom he had never met before, to know a little of himself. He had expressed himself with grace and honesty. I was honored indeed.

As I later read more of Buddy's life and achievements, I was overwhelmed with gratitude for my time with this wise and generous-hearted man.Only a few people would ever have the opportunity to get to know me so intimately. I needed to make sure that I was one of them.

Openly and honestly, in frankness and without fear, Buddy had revealed himself to me. I determined to continue on undaunted, with the lingering sense of Buddy's hand on my chin, searching deeply for who I really was as I fossicked around for remnants of the Italians deep in the heart of my paper bag of life.

With Buddy Rogers at a Variety Club dinner in Palm Springs.

Loving Calder on sight.

CALDER AND CO.

All the sculptors I have ever known are strong—strong of imagination, of heart, of hand, and of arm. They are strong with determination, with passion and sacrifice, and with patience.

As my mind expanded into the life of the Italians in my paper bag of life, I was left doing a fandango with an artist or two of some renown, but only a very few of them were Italian. I worked alongside a number of sculptors, delighted to be welcomed into their worlds to learn about their craft and the sacrifice required. What had captured and brought them into this world of competition and sacrifice, hard work and grime, hope and disappointment, benefactors and detractors? Those who were fortunate enough to have benefactors to pave the way for them worked for years to gain recognition for their work of merit in their world of the tough and dirty work required in order to bring to life such lasting beauty.

DE L'ESPRIE

This beautiful girl was excitement on legs. Every part of her was extravagant and stylish and committed and passionate and fun. We met and worked together over months as she prepared a commission for donors I knew. One more time, I was awed by the darned hard work it takes to be a sculptor. I have watched men's hands and women's hands digging and pulling, bodies straining, pushing and poking and heaving and puffing and panting as they poured out their souls and labored over their craft.

De l'Esprie was everlasting fun, and it was impossible for us to keep our appointments limited to business. So we did not. We shared many intimate hours telling stories of our lives and loves and longings and hopes and dreams. I am grateful for the times we shared.

She is a dark-haired beauty and her very own self who chose her name in order to express to the world who she is and what she is about with her work. "Of the Spirit." Fitting indeed. De l'Esprie has been creating bronze monuments from her Westlake Village Studio for many years. Her works are collected by a list of public figures, celebrities, corporations, and others.

I did so love the meeting of the women sculptors as well as the men. The strength of these women, physically as well as spiritually and mentally, was a challenge and a joy.

Yet I did not think to ask de l'Esprie if her dark good looks could indicate that she was, perhaps, Italian.

With de l'Esprie.

MEHRI DANIELPOUR WEIL

Mehri and all other sculptors I know were "Don't mess with me," kind of folk.

This gracious lady is made of steel. Born in Teheran, Iran, she came to the United States as a small child in 1944. She fell in love with sculpture when she was first exposed to it in Italy.

Mehri is a woman filled with grace. There is a measured peace within her. She is subtle and strong, talented and assured, and in every way a Persian princess. Her work has been collected all over the world and includes commissions by the His Imperial Majesty, the Shah of Iran, and Her Imperial Majesty, Empress Farah of Iran, as well as President Anwar Sadat of Egypt.

As I sat with her discussing the maquette she was preparing for a benefactor, I was washed with the blessing of being in the presence of her talent and her humility.

Mehri uses the lost wax process for the casting of her bronze pieces and loves to capture the personality of her subjects in busts. Her subjects sit for three to four sittings while working at their desks or in other familiar settings. Her sensitive heart causes her to sometimes dream of works, which she sketches out on waking and turns into masterworks.

But gracious and beautiful as she was, Mehri's Persian heritage did little to shed light on the Italians in my paper bag.

With Mehri Danielpour Weil in Palm Springs.

BIG BAD JOHN

He was a bikie. He was big. He was burley. He gave me his red beret when I asked for it. He was strong. He was hairy. He was every inch the picture of a "Big Bad John." He was also a passionately committed sculptor who donated a large portion of his time and work to others. It was my great pleasure to get to know him, and I observed him laboring patiently over his craft for many months—up and down ladders, adjusting, reshaping, finishing. A friend of mine was proud to be one of his benefactors, her breathtaking home filled with many of his works.

A couple who lived in the state of Arizona wished to commission a major work by John in order to donate it to one of their favorite charities. I worked as go-between for months, traversing the red desert, flying back and forth from their home in Arizona to John's studio in Sedona, Arizona. I reveled in getting to know the donors and their joyful generosity, and I reveled in getting to know John and the inspirational power of Sedona. And I reveled in standing in his studio watching him patiently molding in clay what he could see in his mind's eye. He would ask me to stand back and comment, and as I got my eye in slowly, I felt free to observe and suggest as John molded and shaped and poured his creative energies into the clay.

I was overwhelmed toward the end of the process when I was given a privilege of a type I could never have imagined in many years of dreaming.

Once John's magnificent monumental sculpture of Moses was completed in clay and cast in bronze, the donors gave their blessing, and Moses was ready to be shipped to his ultimate destination, where I had arranged a celebratory unveiling. To my humbled surprise, the donors had requested that I should unveil Moses in their stead, as they did not wish to travel so far. So many surprises have tripped me or woken me or frightened me or flattened me as I have trod my path on this earth, but this surprise honored me in a way for which I am ever grateful. It felt big. It still does. It was not only the solemn act. It was the import, the holding of such a responsibility, and the honoring of the generosity of the donors and the gifts and skills of the master craftsman all in one brief moment. I had to hold my breath in wonder.

Unveiling John M. Soderburg's Moses.

With John M. Soderberg, PhD, sculptor.

WYLAND

Wyland is a sculptor as well. A marine-life artist and conservationist particularly enamored of our vast oceans and their creatures, he has inspired millions of people around the world to become passionate stewards of our oceans, lakes, rivers, streams, and wetlands. He has built his business across the United States and the world from a spectacular flagship gallery and studio right on the water at Laguna Beach in California. It was there that he created his first Whaling Wall.

I was invited to the official dedication of the Wyland Building Gallery there along with dozens of guests from many parts of his life, including: Pia Wayne, John Wayne's widow; Keely Shaye Smith, partner of Pierce Brosnan; and Buzz Aldrin. Wyland has been described as "one of the most celebrated artists and conservationists of our time." His massive painted Whaling Walls are on more than one hundred walls in more than sixty-eight countries. This project of Wyland's is one of the largest public arts projects in history, seen by an estimated one billion people each year.

On vacation in California when he was fourteen, Wyland encountered a pair of gray whales while he was swimming in the Pacific Ocean. It was a transformative moment. "I thought that I could call this transformative experience the beginning of the Year of the Whale." He related the memories to me with all the joy and exuberance of a kid still on a mission.

As I write, we in Australia are beset by the mass stranding

of more than 470 pilot whales off the coast of Tasmania, with word that despite heroic efforts, about four hundred of these have died. It is shattering. Marine biologists are scrambling to refloat the remaining beached whales, many of which are on a sandbar near a boat ramp. The reason for such beachings is unknown, although it is known that whales follow a leader and their strong social bonds can lead to whole groups beaching themselves as they make their seasonal migrations in pods as large as one thousand animals. The beached whales in Tasmania called to each other constantly over days as the rescuers toiled to save them, breaking our hearts.

We have an urgent need for Wyland to perform his magic on our shores.

The ineffable ocean. Wyland was drawn to it as a youth and has used his art and great energy to offer the possibility for its healing to the world. In a letter to me he wrote once, "With all the amazing things that have happened I want you to know how much your *ohana* means to me. I look forward to the day when we can get together again for some quality time ... hopefully underwater." He signed off with, "Best fishes and warm aloha." Nothing like a *best fish*, I think to myself. But *underwater*? Not me. Even thinking of it makes me feel claustrophobic. As for ohana, it sounded so lyrically Hawaiian (and I love that place) that I checked to discover that it refers to "a person's extended family." But not much of my Italian extended family were anywhere I could see in Wyland's spectacular work. Too bad.

BUZZING AROUND

Buzz was Buzz.

Gemini XII and Apollo 11 astronaut and moonwalker; West Point; USAF Colonel, Korean War Vet; MIT ScD; Human Space Fight Institute founder Dr. Buzz Aldrin is also sometimes known as Dr. Rendevous. An American former astronaut, engineer, and fighter pilot, he made three spacewalks as pilot of the 1966 Gemini mission and as the lunar module pilot of the 1969 Apollo 11 mission. His total of five and a half hours of walking in space proved that human beings can function effectively in the vacuum of space. A Presbyterian elder, Buzz was the first person to hold a religious ceremony on the moon when he privately took communion after landing near the edge of Mare Tranquillitatis.

I do love the fact that his given name was Edwin Eugene Aldrin Jr., and that because his sister Fay Ann could not say the word "brother," he became known as Buzzer or Buzz.

He is a hero. What else can I say about such a man? As the second person to walk on the moon, he had been taking his historic step while I was sinking slowly to the floor in my apartment in Salem, Massachusetts, overtired and unwell with my first pregnancy. Instead of clapping and cheering him on his way across the surface of the moon I had slept my way through that event. I was very sad about that but chose not to tell him when we met.

Buzz was charming and relaxed. In the moments we had

together, as much as I exerted my imagination, I knew it was impossible for me to ever experience what he must have thought and the awe and wonder he must have felt as he viewed our blue planet, the Blue Marble, from the moon. I was so happy simply to be near to a man of such accomplishment that I was caught grinning away with something akin to the grin I displayed when I was trying to out-grin Carol Channing.

"Best fishes" from Wyland.

With Buzz Aldrin at the opening of the Wyland Building Gallery at Laguna Beach.

Buzz served as the lunar module pilot for the historic Apollo 8 flight and was put in charge of creating docking and rendezvous techniques for spacecraft and pioneered underwater training techniques to simulate spacewalking. The photograph he took of himself while on a space flight with the Gemini XII is now called the first "selfie" in space. He was awarded the Presidential Medal of Freedom and has the Aldrin Crater on the moon named after him.

I have Buzz's signature on a card proclaiming the Official

Dedication of the Wyland Building and am quietly proud to own this piece of history. His hand touched mine as he signed, and one more time I felt like the proverbial girl in the song, "I've danced with a man, who's danced with a girl, who's danced with the Prince of Wales." My hand had touched the hand of an American hero, the second man to step onto the moon. I felt for a brief moment that I was only one small step from stepping onto the moon myself. Buzz was a superstar, and I was touched by his humanity and quietly pleased that I met him after all, despite sleeping my way through his historic step onto the moon. "Standing on the lunar surface for the first time is a memory I'll treasure forever," said Buzz. Sharing a few precious moments in conversation with him at Wyland's studio and gallery is a moment I will treasure forever.

Enlightenment again? It has been revealed to us mere mortals recently that radiation levels measured on the moon are about two hundred times higher than on the surface of the earth. If I tried hard enough, I could almost convince myself that the 200 percent extra radiation on the moon may have reflected from Buzz's smiling self across to me, wiping out the jot and tittle of my Italian spittle and leaving me bereft.

I remember Buzz's descriptions as he recalled, "Beautiful view, magnificent desolation." Perhaps this is part of the answer to the mystery of the disappearance of the Italians in my paper bag. It behooves me to remember to be much more thoughtful about the folk I stand close to. Perhaps a shield would help, or even a Covid mask.

Life had been transformative for Buzz. Who but his fellow

astronauts could begin to comprehend what Buzz had seen, what he had experienced, what he had felt, what he had thought, or what he had longed for on his return to Earth? He states that upon his return he felt isolated, alone, and uncertain. He had made a quantum leap. I who have been all my life bound to the earth, have also found myself isolated, alone, and uncertain on the edge of my own quantum leaps. I too can be threatened by the life that I am called to live, after the life I have known.

By the way, did you know that Buzz's mother's maiden name was Moon? 'Nuff said.

Buzz Aldrin's autograph on Wyland.

SHARING BIRTHDAYS

With Buzz and Pia and Wyland and others hovering in the background at Wyland's celebration, Keely Shaye Smith and I fell into a natural conversation about life and love and hope and disappointment, and shared some blessed moments of laughter. Her partner, Pierce Brosnan, was unable to come to the gathering, which greatly disappointed me, as I wanted one closeup glimpse of the cheeky grin on his beautiful face.

As we chatted, Keely told me that her babe was due on January 16. At that I stood amazed, probably with my mouth agape. "That is my birthday!" I gasped in disbelief, and we laughed again as we stood together enjoying the pleasure of each other's company. When Keely and Pierce married in Ireland at Ballintubber Castle, I was cheering. Pierce had formerly been married to an Australian girl. There had been much sorrow in his life, and now his "brown-eyed beauty" was by his side.

With Keeley Shaye Smith, enjoying a laugh or two and an unexpected Australian connection.

No matter how hard I looked at her beautiful face I could detect no connection to Italy within the charming girl named Keely Shaye Smith, and I thus did not seek her comment on the Italians in my paper bag. We spoke of babies and Australia and life and loves and were happy to enjoy each other's company and a few moments of shared laughter there at Wyland's gallery in Laguna.

RIBBON CUTTER

Lloyd Bridges was there too. I loved the sound of his full name, Lloyd Verdet Bridges Jr. I had been delighted to read that he had won the winner's cup in a fat-baby contest but chose not to remind him of that. He was known as an athletic actor, popular for his underwater work as an ex-Navy frogman. He became a small-screen star of giant proportions when he starred in *Sea Hunt* and had appeared in more than 150 feature films. He was father of four sons, one of whom, Jeff Bridges, states with a smile that his father was, "so full of life and so joyous." I also knew that he frequently acted with his sons Beau and Jeff.

He seemed to me to be one of the world's good guys, all blue-eyed sparkle and good humor, and proved himself to be a champion ribbon cutter. But as his parents were of English stock, I could not ask any of my Italian questions there.

I was beginning to live with disappointment in my mouth.

With Lloyd Verdet Bridges at the opening of Wyland's gallery in Laguna.

Pia Pallette Wayne also joined in Wyland's celebration. A Peruvian actress who had married John Wayne (twenty-one years her senior) in 1954, she was still extremely beautiful, although she came across as somewhat aloof.

All the folk celebrating at the gallery with Wyland were accomplished, charming, interesting, and unique in their own way, but none was Italian—at least that I could tell. My joy on that day was in being with them and not in attempting to unlock their store of untold tales whispered down through generations with Italian pride.

AN ITALIAN AT LAST

Until one bright and shining California day, from the House of Fontanini in the village of Bagni di Lucca, Italy, came a fourth-generation member of the house of Fontanini which is known for its creation of magnificent nativities. Oh, and was he gorgeous! Visiting California on business, Emanuele Fontanini was as beautifully attractive in personality as both his name and his heritage. I could easily have left everything and run away with him to Lucca or any other place he might have mentioned. But he did not mention anything.

The House of Fontanini is well known for producing products that they proudly suggest have the characteristics of warmth, sincerity, love, and passion—and the gorgeous Emanuele was the personification of all this. The Fontanini Company has kept to the old tradition of Lucchesi figurines since 1908, when it was established by Emanuele Fontanini Sr., who worked with the finest painters and sculptors in Tuscany.

The original Emanuele died in 1977 at the great age of ninety-seven. This is the age at which my great-grandfather Antonio Capuano Pavarno died in Creswick, Victoria, Australia. Antonio was also considered to be "of a great age."

And Lucca? This charming northern Italian city is where I stayed on my very first visit to Italy. There it was that I felt my Italian blood racing in recognition. I was *home* and I knew it. I felt a connection to all the people who hurried past me on their way to shop or cook, to gossip over *un caffè*, or to enjoy the sights and sounds of historic Lucca. After all, I was part Italian, wasn't I?

I still held that sense of deep belonging in my heart when I met Emanuele. But we were busy with business, and I did not ask him one question about the Italians in my paper bag. Too bad.

With Emanuele Fontanini from Bagni di Lucca. A bit of a likeness there?

LORENZO

With a name like Lorenzo, it was my guess even before I met him that he was of Italian heritage. With his family name of Ghiglieri it helped to cement that idea into my mind. And so, he was.

Good friends of mine were benefactors of his, and I enjoyed the privilege of a flight with them to his home and studio in Oregon. Lorenzo had been born in Los Angeles to a sculptor

father and a French pianist and vocalist mother. Highly energetic and prolific, he was named as "one of the world's best-rec-
ognized and most successful sculptors and artists."

Thus, with what I still believed to be my Italian heritage,
we had a connection and enjoyed many hours as he explained
his work to me over the next few months. Lorenzo's work is
as gentle as a breeze and as profound as the earth, and his
life force is passionately displayed. His canvases are filled with
both anguish and beauty. His work reaches out, drawing you
into his dreaming. No wonder it is prized by both royalty and
aristocrats.

Lorenzo had many girlfriends, he told me later, but really
wanted me for himself. That was a surprise. Perhaps it was an
Italian surprise. There was no lead-in to that conversation. But
the Italian connection was not enough, and he continued to
paint and sculpt and be successful and well recognized while I
got on with my life. Lorenzo also told me that I had a mind like
a pinball machine. Perhaps I do. I never did ask him to explain
himself further. Was that, too, an Italian characteristic?

PHILOSOPHY

Another gentleman with whom I worked looked at me quizzi-
cally one day and told me that I had an, "impertinent intelligence." Where did that come from, and how long had he been
thinking that way? Perhaps that was an Italian characteristic.

Our local Greek dry cleaner told me that I was a philoso-
pher. "You must be Greek," he laughed at me. And here I was,

busily hunting down the Italians in my paper bag? What a paradox. The brain of a female is usually matured by the age of twenty-one, I read. Perhaps mine had come into maturity a little late. But I had been informed somewhere along the way in my life that "hope is taking action," and I was not about to allow such comments to deter me in my hunt for the Italians in my paper bag.

With Lorenzo Ghiglieri in Portland, Oregon.

RIDERLESS HORSE

Risk and chance are constants in the story of my life. Mr.T and I accepted an invitation to a small celebration in our apartment building. It was at the beginning of another spring, with all its offerings of hope and renewal. Nothing could have prepared me for the result of that casual acceptance. I could never have conjured up from my imagination the results of a chance meeting there.

Glass of wine in hand, I was gleaning threads of stories from the lives of people around me in a room abuzz with quiet chatter and the making of new acquaintances. Behind me I heard the flutter of a gentle American accent. Intrigued, I slipped away from my group to attach myself to that voice. The smile I received in response to my question was compelling. "Are you from the USA or Canada?" I asked. I had learned enough in my years in both of those countries not to ever presume I knew. "I'm from California," said a fresh-faced beauty as she welcomed me to join her. "That is my other home," I replied, happy with this unexpected turn of events. "I lived there for six years. Which part of California are you from?" I asked.

She smiled her pleasure and said that I would probably never have heard of Hope College. Oh yes, I had, I assured her. I knew the president there and had visited with him a few times. Now the fresh-faced beauty gasp-spluttered her disbelief. Opening her mouth, she gasped out, "That is my father!"

We spluttered and splattered our laughter and disbelief from her husband to mine and eventually to the rest of the guests. It was surely not possible? She was newly in Australia, having married an Armenian Australian, and had moved into our silo building. I was newly married and in living back in Australia, having moved back from Florida to marry a man I had known in my youth and had not seen or spoken with in forty years—up until recently that is. This was a moment of small miracles.

From that first meeting we moved on to a gentle burgeoning of friendship, and one day she told me that she would soon turn fifty, and to mark her special day she and her husband were making plans to spend a few weeks in Siena, Tuscany. Such was her eager anticipation that she had already arranged a Sienese tour guide who was able to offer far more than was available on the general tourist run. The trip was to be arranged to coincide with her family's and friends' vacations. She and her husband would be pleased if we would like to join them. Would we like to join them? "Oh yes! Thank you!" was my eager reply in all of two seconds. I was instantly determined to take on that challenge and join her celebration.

When I had first heard of *Il Palio di Siena* some years before, it placed itself right onto my to-do list with not a bit of help from me. It sat right up there at the top along with a visit to see the Northern Lights and visit the Red Center of Australia. Ever since, it stayed in my imagination, spinning color and noise as days and weeks and years went by.

And then I was invited and went to that little celebratory party to welcome spring, and there I ran smack bang into a beautiful Californian girl whose father was the president of Hope college, and who was married to an Australian Armenian man, and who now lived in Melbourne town in our apartment building. And there we were, laughing in disbelief, and there I was, saying that of course we would join her and her family and friends in Siena for her fiftieth birthday celebration and the racing of Il Palio di Siena.

I treasured the thought of it. Suddenly I was preparing to enter into a world of my imagination come to life with all the flamboyance of Italy at its superstar best. The floodlights shone bright into my imagination. But nothing could have prepared me for the floodlights of Siena's preparations for the running of Il Palio, where I felt I was moved onto another planet. In that special place I thrilled in ecstasy along with the Italians who were rustling around in my paper bag.

With a Sienese stunner in *LUPA Contrada* while I still believed I was two-sixteenth Italian. We are wearing our LUPA scarves especially made for the occasion.

Held twice every year, Il Palio di Siena involves ten horses and their bareback riders dressed in appropriate colors and chosen from ten of the seventeen *contrade*. Hordes of over-zealous Italian men are said to try to help their horses win the famous race by kissing the horses on the lips. I cannot vouch for these moments of animation as I did not witness them, but then—who am I to say? The race lasts no more than ninety seconds, and it is common for a few jockeys to be thrown from their horses while maneuvering the treacherous turns in the piazza. Il Palio di Siena runs for three laps of the Piazza del Campo, on the steeply canted track where the perimeter is covered for safety purposes with several inches of protective dirt and tuff, a light porous rock lithified from volcanic ash.

All horses are of mixed breed with no purebred horse allowed. Amazingly, a horse can win without its rider because the race is won by the horse who represents his *contrada*, and not by the jockey. Il Palio di Siena is preceded by a spectacular two-hour pageant known as the *Coreo Storico* with flag wavers wearing medieval costumes. This formally choreographed triumphal march commemorates the ancient institutions and customs of the Republic of Siena.

There are as many as seven hundred participants in the parade, with visitors coming from around the world to revel in the spectacle. Public races in Siena have their origins in medieval times.

The Palio itself is a seven-foot-tall, painted, silk banner bearing a new design created each year. This is the trophy for the winning contrada. The contrade are seventeen districts within the city of Siena. Each contrada is named after an animal or is a symbol with a long and complicated history, including heraldic and semi-mythological associations. In Siena the contrade were originally set up during the Middle Ages to preserve the city's independence from Florence. Every contrada has its own museum, church, fountain, baptismal font, and motto.

Our guide offered us the unusual privilege of entering the inner sanctum of the *Contrada Lupa*, which means she-wolf. Legend has it that this contrada was founded by Senius and Aschius, the sons of Remus who were raised by a wolf. Lupa's sister city is Rome. We feasted there with hundreds of the Contrada Lupa's members, who were mad with excitement about the forthcoming race. We were invited into the inner sanctum of their museum, where we were knocked breathless by the displays of ancient costumes and flags, as well as exquisite furnishings of all kinds. We watched the beautifully elegant horses being led through the city prior to the running of the race. We drank wine especially labeled for Contrada Lupa.

The itinerary offered was exotic. I was about to be transported to Italian heaven, right into the lap of my Italian history. I was very happy.

On the thirteenth of August we were to meet our guide at the Porte Ovile gate and visit the horse assignment in Piazza del Campo.

Lunch would follow at Ristorante Compagnia dei Vinattieri. From there it was suggested that we watch the contradas enter the square for the first trial. This, we were told, would be quite intense. On the fifteenth of August we were to be in Siena for the trial, and then to have dinner at Contrada Lupa. The sixteenth was to be the running of the Palio, and we had tickets. Following the race, we were to visit the *duomo* to see the celebrations and enjoy dinner inside the Piazza del Campo. Our grand finale.

But, and how can I say this without wiping a tear from my eye? Mr. T loved the thought of tool kits for old Porsches far more than the thought of watching Il Palio di Siena live. And we did not use our tickets. And I did not see the running of Il Palio. It came about like this.

In the ancient city of Perugia, an 89-kilometer drive south from Siena, there lived a fine-looking Italian gentleman who had been a racing car driver of some renown in his youth. Mr. T and he had met online over a Porsche tool kit or two of such rarity that meeting him in his hometown could not be put off, even until the day after the racing of Il Palio. I was devastated. No matter which way I looked at it, I could not understand the pull of any tool kit, no matter how rare. But Mr. T was adamant, and I wept my goodbyes and bundled into our hired car with my grief.

Perugia was another Italian historic marvel, and we were well looked after. I looked on as Mr. T and Mr. Perugia negotiated over tool kits with their heads deep inside the trunk of a car as the horses ran in Siena. Money was exchanged, and they were both very happy.

And one more time, I lived with disappointment in my mouth as we traveled back to Australia with a rare Porsche tool kit in Mr. T's luggage. Treasure indeed.

The Italians in my paper bag were very quiet.

Our tickets for Il Palio. Unused.

FARREN-PRICE ON A PARK BENCH

The very first time I visited Italy it was with my sister Anne Miree and brother-in-law Thomas, who had already reveled in much travel in and about northern Italy. They knew the terrain well, and so, "Lucca!" they had demanded when it was decided that I would join them for a month. "Let's all go to Lucca. It is our favorite place in Italy." And go we did.

They used their many contacts to arrange a perfect cottage for us to rent.

Perched on a hill overlooking the fourteenth-century clock tower of the city, it was situated at about a thirty-minute drive out of Lucca. The "dwelling" had all the look of a rather wearily enlarged hen house, but the daubed stone and crumbling bits and pieces were offset by a charming pergola, under which we sipped our wine and pretended to be sophisticated in every European way.

Having been born in Eindhoven, in the Netherlands, and having migrated to Australia and then later to the United States, Thomas moved into full European mode the moment we stepped from the plane in Milan. He walked in a different way, and his elegant musician's hands and his face all took on the subtle elegance of a European. There was something in that air, and he could smell it.

Never having been to Italy, I was agog as I followed along tugging my suitcase. From Milan we took the train to Lucca, a journey of about three and a half hours, and I pleasured myself looking at the rolling countryside. I was in Italy at last.

It had been arranged that we would be picked up at the Lucca railway station by a gentleman who would drive us up the hill to our cottage, leaving us with the car that belonged to the owners of that cottage, and who were happy for us to rent it as well. Off the train we found ourselves on a very long platform inside an elegant nineteenth-century building. I was sure that we had stepped onto a movie set. I was sensing the European fragrance that Thomas was responding to. I was *home*.

After some wandering up and down the platform, and with no evidence of our car and driver, Anne Miree began to show her agitation, and Thomas began to try his telephone to see if he could hasten the driver to our rescue. Thomas's hands moved constantly as he talked, and from time to time he pushed back his hair with elegant musician's fingers as his frustration grew. Beside him, Anne Miree continued to admonish him, chirping her advice while he batted her away as he attempted to concentrate on his conversation in limited Italian. As there was little I could do to be of assistance, I wandered off outside the station to wait. There I did wait. And wait. And wait. An hour or two went by while I sat dreamily breathing in pure Italian air. Neither the man nor the car appeared.

Thomas and Anne Miree moved further and further into sorting-it-out mode, finally using the telephone booth to chase up our errant man. Two were enough playing at that game, and as I had no ability to help with the Italian language,

I wandered across to a small park in the nearby square sited on the edge of the city center to occupy myself with more waiting. The sky was a clear blue and the square was filled with the twitter of birds. I sat myself down comfortably on a bench and was drinking in "the Italian bit," when a fine-looking gentleman came quietly up from behind me as if from nowhere and sat down beside me. By now I was certain that I had landed on a movie set. It was a moment of utter magic.

He ran a hand across his patrician brow and smiled invitingly. His appearance was benign, and he was such charming company that we soon fell into chatting about life. It took me not more than a minute to realize a little sadly that he was not going to be one of the Italians in my paper bag. Of all the impossibly improbable things, he was an Australian. There was a moment or two as we contemplated each other in astonishment. I could discern a worldliness and chivalry in my companion. I was aware of sophistication and civility, yet I could hardly take in the incongruity of our situation.

My first time in Italy. My first time in Lucca. Me sitting waiting for a car that was not appearing. Thomas trying to find out what had happened. Anne Miree chirping instructions. No stationmaster in sight. No one in sight. And suddenly I was sitting next to an Australian who had appeared out of nowhere to sit by my side in a small park by the railway station in Lucca. We laughed together over the impossible coincidence, and he expressed his pleasure at seeing that I was adventuring into Lucca for the first time, as it was a city that he loved and which he believed would bring me much joy. He introduced himself using his family name of Farren-Price. I puzzled a little at this name. Then, "I am Ronald," he said as he introduced himself further. It sounded vaguely familiar. Then, "Yes," he nodded smiling in answer to my question; he was a part of the well-known family of the House of Farren-Price, jewelers of distinction in Australia. By the end of our conversation, we were chatting like old acquaintances, and he shared with me that he was a pianist currently resident in Genoa, and with that he rose waving his elegant hand and bade me farewell. I had been gifted with a treasured moment of joy there in Lucca, sitting in the Piazza Ricasoli in front of the Porta San Pietro outside the railway station. I was pleasured much by the gift of our unexpected meeting. I have no photographs of those moments but the pictures remain in my mind, clear and bright with joy. When Mr. Farren-Price and his wife walked past the three of us the next day as we sat enjoying Lucca food and sunshine, he waved to me as though we were old friends. All that Italian blood surged in my veins. I was indeed home.

I was later to learn much more of Ronald Farren-Price's outstanding career as a concert pianist of renown and a music educator. He remains a "charming and much-loved vital presence in the Melbourne music scene." He is considered "a legend of Australian music." And again, he is described as "being completely infused with the great music he plays and loves, and has fully absorbed all its wisdom and generosity." But for that moment under the Italian sun, we were two Australians meeting in an unexpected way in an unexpected place.

By the time Thomas and Anne Miree had finished their telephoning, we all had stories to share.

SKIDDING AND SKUDDING

The missing driver who had in his grasp our missing car had mistakenly thought that we three were arriving in Lucca the day before. Finding himself to be running late, he had put his foot down a little too hard in the tiny blue car and, racing down the hill and around the hairpin bends on the rutted dusty road, he had skidded, tipped the car on its side, and continued to skid down the hill on his side for some time before he came to a halt. Safe but mightily shaken by his experience, he righted the car with local help and continued carefully down the hill into Lucca in the sadly battered blue automobile. Once safely at the Lucca railway station he waited and waited for us while recovering his equanimity, just as we had waited and waited for him while losing ours.

One innocuous digit made such an enormous difference. He had come to Lucca railway station one day early. Only one. How much we can miss in life by just one step, or one hour, or one glance, or one call, or one kiss. He had the time of our arrival correct but the date a tad wrong.

To this day I do not know who was at fault. But at this moment on this day, as Thomas was delving into the mystery of his nonappearance, he was busily occupied and unable to make the trip all the way down the hill again. We would need to find our own way up to our rented cottage where he would meet up with us later. This turn of events left us considering our three heavy suitcases with neither a car nor a bus in sight, and collectively daunted by the thought of the long, long walk up the hill to our cottage. We were now left standing abandoned under the blue skies and the burnished Italian sun. We lacked the ability to change our situation and there was no one in sight who could come to the aid of three, weary, jilted Australians. What we needed was to mount up with wings like eagles.

Scraps of conversation in a mixture of Italian, English, and German wafted across the lawn as Miree and I watched Thomas attempt our rescue. Following another hour or two of determined telephone talk, a taxi flew right into the square in place of an eagle, landing with a skid in front of our luggage. We were quick to bundle ourselves in, and as we set off up the hill I listened in fascination as German became the common language between the taxi driver and Thomas. Thomas is of Dutch origin and could not speak much Italian, and the taxi driver who was Italian could not speak much English, so German it was. They eventually worked out a system of communication between them and on we drove with Anne Miree interrupting to inform us all about her suggested methods of travel on the back roads of Lucca. The taxi driver smiled thinly, indicating that he knew what he was doing. I sat quietly amused and hoped he knew where it was that we were to go, and that Thomas and he had made a good alliance in their elementary German.

On and on and on, on the dusty narrow roads we wound

our way up—now quickly, now slowly—as we passed through tiny village after tiny village. We were slowing up to creep around one more sharp curve and past a few cottages, with Thomas gesticulating at the driver, when there was a loud banging on one of the side windows. What on earth? The taxi driver skidded and stuttered the car to an abrupt and angry halt, dust flying. Then there was more gesticulating going on outside than inside, so down with the window and ready with an expletive or two the taxi driver started to yell. He was looking grim with his brow furrowed, and his fist was in the air. His foot revving the accelerator in irritation, he was preparing to move us on again when, with her hands to her face, Anne Miree cried out in impassioned surprise to the gesticulating young woman standing beside the taxi, "What on earth are *you* doing here?"

It was far past the possible. Now laughing, now crying, Anne Miree jumped out of the taxi and she and the lass who had banged so hard on the window hugged and kissed and generally behaved like long-lost sisters.

What they were was a couple of old friends from San Diego. The beautiful girl I was now meeting by the side of a dusty road in a tiny village outside of Lucca had fallen in love with an outrageously handsome Italian gent a few years before, and as any self-respecting girl should, had married him. Off she raced with him to live an exotic life in Lucca. He had thrown her over his shoulder and carted her off to this miniscule village, as any self-respecting Italian gentleman should. And there, as our taxi slowed and we were creeping past their home, which was situated right on the side of the road, she happened to be standing outside. And she spotted Anne Miree through the window. Talk about "you in your small corner and I in mine."

Life is full of surprises. Including Italian ones.

ON A BLANKET

In that wonderful city of Lucca, the gentleman who had slipped sideways down the hill in a small blue car in an effort to meet us one day too early ultimately became our guide and very friendly neighbor. He had found his way to Lucca from his home in England some years before and was happily living on the side of a hill overlooking the city. When we were invited to his home for dinner, we gladly accepted. We sat together as the sun set and the lights of the city twinkled their greeting to the night sky. He had set up a table for four in his vineyard. There we sat breathing in Italian paradise in the mellow evening. It was a place in which you could lie down and die without a regret. The table was candlelit and the wine he served was of his own vinification and from his own vines. My life had now expanded out into far more than the city of Lucca as I mellowed into a setting fit for the gods of all things Italian.

My joy was filled to overflowing when our host told us that as well as being a vintner, he was a ballet dancer, and that if we were so inclined, we could follow him down the hill on the next Sunday to watch him dance in the *Piazza San Michele*. This was his weekend routine and passion. Smiling in answer to our query about why we should follow him down the hill when he could ride with us after all in the battered little blue car, he went to the rear of his house and reappeared with a bicycle. Attached to the back was an ungainly homemade caboose, the oddest contraption I had ever seen. "Guess what this is for?" he grinned at me as he handled it tenderly. I could not. The only thing I could think of was that it looked something like an extra wide skateboard. "That," he exclaimed, all dimples and delight, "is exactly what it is."

Each weekend for the past few years he had loaded a long black boom box onto his caboose-cum-skateboard and with great care had wound his way down the dusty, rutted roads and into the Piazza San Michele. There in the square amidst a tempest of traders and tourists he laid out a blanket, turned up the volume of his boom box, and poured out his heart as he danced with all the pride and extravagance of a ballerino dancing at La Scala in Milan. His extravagant magic was unleashed in sight of the Chiesa di San Michele in Foro, the Roman Catholic basilica built over the ancient Roman forum, and until 1370 the seat of the *Consiglio Maggiore*, the commune's most important assembly. Incongruous? Yes. Italian? Yes, also. I loved it all.

CLAIM PEGGING

The more I go on with all this Italian business, the more my mind clears and I see at last that the one and only drop of Italian I could ever have laid claim to was in the name,

Capuano-Pavarno. The funny thing is that I did not know I had laid claim to anything until I sent off my tittle of spittle.

My childhood was not filled with reminiscences of "the Old Country." We did not sit at our table in a swirl of tales of the Italian rellies and their doings. My step-grandmother Isabella McGregor Murchie Capuano Pavarno told me not one thing about her Italian husband, Francis Capuano Pavarno. Nor did she keep so much as one photograph of him anywhere amongst the Scottish "doings" she had brought with her on her long journey to Melbourne from Darvel in Scotland. It cannot have been much of a love match. I heard not one word about the only husband she ever had? I saw not one photograph? Married to Francis Capuano Pavarno at the age of thirty-two and a dressmaker by profession, she was entirely the Scot for as long as I knew her. She bore Francis no children. It seemed that not much of the Italian spittle had splattered across to mix with her Scottish DNA.

So it is that I mull over this paper bag of my life and the Italians who have occupied it with me, and I am a little sad. There was a hole in my bucket all along. I had simply not seen it before. Nothing was leaking out. Nothing was ever there. At least not much. A name. And that is all. And even that had needed some clarification. The two-sixteenths Italian DNA I thought I could claim was "it." I could not even doll myself up in regalia as spectacular as Phil Stevens's, and he—only three-eighteenths Sioux. Nothing had leaked out. The DNA-gods were either wrong or they were right. And whatever they offered me after the analysis of my little tittle of spittle was all I would get.

BOWLED OVER

It was not an Italianate but a Japanese-styled home in the midst of Atlanta, Georgia that became a fascination to me. I was privileged to be the guest of the generous and privileged couple who lived there. As together we explored their gardens that had been created to bring the serenity of Japanese expertise into their home via huge windows, I felt a great opening of my spirit. The home was serene, elegant, secluded, and filled with beauty.

Of all their treasures, the most unusual and spellbinding for me was a set of large, rounded, wooden bowls so darkly buffed and polished that they had an inner glow as of amber. I wanted to touch them. I wanted to leave them alone. I wanted to hold them close to me. I wanted to keep my distance. They had been placed on the floor strategically near the entrance door so that to observe them well, it was necessary to bend or kneel.

These treasures were sculpture of a different kind. I have never again seen anything so profound. Carved by a gentleman who had been an architect in his former life, they were paper-thin, simple and elegant, and looked both as light as air and as profound as the earth. Fine, strong, smooth and mind-absorbing, I coveted them. I remember them, and I covet them still. The wood deemed necessary for the carving of these treasures was carved from huge trees and soaked in a special solution for two months before it was ready to be carved. The bowls were so light they were almost translucent as they sat presiding over all the goings and comings by the door, unmissable.

They reached out to me through the space and freedom of that home, stretching through time without a word, connecting my soul and spirit to something eternal. I felt a deep joy as I contemplated them. They caused me to think of the ecstasy of watching Nureyev dance, or of reading Dostoyevsky. I felt the connect, connect, connect ticking down through time to touch me. I felt connected to the hand and heart of the architect who had fashioned them. They brought with them the breath of God. They took my breath away.

MAGIC

Carol Channing also took my breath away. She was magic on wheels and as dazzling in person as she was on the stage where she sang her heart out with legs flying for the joy of living and entertaining. I wanted to laugh every minute at the verve and dynamism she tossed across the stage to her audience as she sang out "Hello, Dolly!" as though she loved us. Age had neither wearied nor daunted her.

Following her brilliant performance, we were introduced by Rhonda Fleming, and in our photograph together the reflected sparkles from her dress sprinkle me all over with stardust, a glittering image of her magnetism and personal drive. She was as funny in person as she was on stage, and as we chatted and laughed for the camera, I worked up some of my DNA and tried my best to out-smile her. But try as I might, she won hands down. Along with the sparkles that shower me like confetti and the bursting generosity of her smile, Carol was holding tight to a glass of champagne. Of course! Bubbles for the biggest, brightest, bubbliest person of them all, who once revealed that she was emotionally drawn to the stage after seeing Ethel Waters perform. Oh yes.

Carol's heritage was African American, German, and German Jewish, and she said that she knew it was true the moment she began to sing and dance, and that she was as proud as can be of her ancestry. But I did not ask her more. Years later I was gifted with a DNA analysis which in turn caused me to reflect on my heritage and the variety of people I had met in my life. I was blessed one more time with the knowledge that we are all one.

We of this earth: Italian or German, Irish or Japanese, artistic or musical, literary or Swedish, Lithuanian or Sudanese, tall or short—we are part of the same, living, breathing universe and of the family of man.

Griff always told me to, "Gear up." So I geared up with Carol and offered my best grin for the camera, but no matter how I tried, there was no way to match the shining joyful face of the one and only Carol Channing.

I thought of the extravagance of the author Barbara Cartland when I met Carol. Barbara wrote a remarkable 723 novels during her lifetime and is said to have deliberately played the role of Grande Dame to the hilt with her big hair, jewels, white fox furs, and her trademark pink chiffon. "The color," she said, "helps you to be clever." I must agree. Go Barbara! Go Carol! Go Jillian!

Trying to out-grin the stunning Carol Channing while doused in the confetti of her sparkles.

MISSING MY CUE

Fluffed up and shining as brightly as I could, I took to my trusty Merc for one more flying visit up the freeway to the Dorothy Chandler Pavilion in Los Angeles to enjoy a concert by the Australian pianist David Helfgott, in which he was to present us with Rachmaninov's enormously demanding Piano Concerto No. 3, accompanied by the Hollywood Bowl Orchestra. David's complex life had been portrayed in the movie Shine, in which he is played by the Australian actor Jeffrey Rush, who was awarded Best Actor for this role at the 69th Academy Awards. Concert over, I joined David and his wife as well as His Excellency the Australian Ambassador to the United States and a few others for a celebratory drink or two. I had spent some time talking with Scott Hicks, the director of the movie *Shine*, and a number of other interesting folk, when toward the end of the evening I found myself standing beside a tall woman who seemed vaguely familiar. I introduced myself with, "Good evening. My name is Jillian. I am sorry, I do not know your name."

There was a moment of disbelieving silence followed by an impatient intake of breath by my tall companion. This was followed by a straightening of her back, a stiffening of her spine, and a haughty look down her patrician nose. "I am Lynn Redgrave," she breathed over me. One more time in this town of learning to "be somebody," I had tripped over my own feet in an effort to be polite. "How could you not have known?"

she inferred, imperious and unyielding to my discomfort as I valiantly endeavored to keep down my mirth. After all she was somebody, and who was I? Who was I that I did not recognize her immediately? Who was I not to pay obeisance? How dare I? I had met this look and this type of reaction before in the glitzy world of Tinsel Town. If you know yourself to be somebody, all surrounding beings had jolly well better be *en garde*.

With Scott Hicks, director of the Australian movie *Shine*.

DREAMS

They say to write them down.
The dreams.
Write them down and you will remember them.
It just may be
that given time for reflection and rumination,
understanding will result.

Understanding of what?
Long lost loves?
The riddles of the universe?
Where I left the key to the back door?

It makes sense.
It seems simple enough
and could even be a good idea,
or a very good idea.
Dream writing.

I remember what they say
as I prepare my knackered self for sleep.
"Good idea.
Write them down,"
I whisper to myself.
But as the morning wakens me,
the bluster of life-preserving activity
takes hold with a vengeance.
Eyedrops blinker life into focus.
Breathe in. Breathe out.
Like the blonde.
The one you remember
who went to the hairdresser wearing headphones?
"Do not remove these," she said,
pointing.

Wash and rinse. Color, wash and rinse again. Condition. Dry.
Brush.

It was all too hard.
As the blonde melted into glossy magazines
the hairdresser removed her headphones.
The blonde dropped over.
Dead.
Stone cold dead.
What to do?
Listen to headphones for a clue?
And there it was.
"Breathe in, breathe out."

Here I stand,
searching for my dreams.

Once I was a child astride a golden horse,
hair flying,
fulsome laughter.
Fulsome life
begging my body forward
into unknowable dreams.
I would live forever,
unsullied by grief.

But my dreams today
are waking dreams,

not spent in the back alleys of my mind.
As I slumber,
I dream with love
of the lives of my children,
and my children's children.

For I have seen winter dreams.
I have seen him on his knees
begging for money.
An old man then,
silver of hair,
craggy of feature,
bereft
of the salve for his cravings.

Winter.
I have seen this.
Winter dreams with leaden skies.
Trees
stripped bare of the glory of their autumn foliage.
Gray highways
clothed only in the slush
of dreams of riven snow.
Wind chill.
Forty degrees below.
Winter in Chicago.
I have seen this.

Youth is for dreaming.
Young men shall dream dreams,
and those of great good fortune
shall find someone to encourage their dreams.
While we,
at the gate of the winter of our lives,
adjust our dreams.

We give and receive,
give and receive,
and give and receive again.
We cradle our children and our children's children.
We breathe into their nostrils
the fresh air of hope
for their dreams.
They,
with the new sap of spring rising,
will warm us with their dreams,
these children of spring.

In this vast land of hope
there is room enough
for all our dreaming.
This winter is not the end.
For winter offers dreams
of
spring,
of hope,

and of new life.

I blink and turn myself,
look boldly into the mirror and say,
"Go girl. You go, girl. You can do it.
Write them down.
Your dreams."

HORIZON HUNTERS

On one return trip to Australia from the United States I
stopped off at my favorite watering hole, Hawaii. Despite the
Italian bit, I was born to be an island girl. I was always a bit
of a hothouse plant. Being one to explore, I took a bus to the
Maritime Museum in Honolulu. "A bus!" expostulated Griff,
amused at my temerity. Of the people who were on the bus
with me, each one had old eyes and hollow cheeks. Each carried a plastic bag filled with food. Each wore colorful clothing.
Where were they going and what were they dreaming on this
day as I was looking for their Maritime Museum and more
adventures? As I read now that the museum closed in 2009
"due to economic constraints," I am wearied by those who
could not see the transformative value of the treasures inside.

Once through the front door, their slant on information
about Captain James Cook offered me a connection to his
brilliant career as a navigator—and to Australia in a curious
and unexpected way. He and I were old acquaintances now
meeting on Ouahu. I moved on through the museum and was

transported into a world of such startling revelation that the grace of its memory is with me still, a marker in my life even up to now.

Hiding in a tight little corner of the museum, sitting quietly in diffuse light, was a video machine I could play it if I wanted. And I wanted. There was not another soul in sight as I stood quietly and in awe.

All that I saw on that small video, all that was said and all that was not said, I wanted to hold in my hand, in my mind, in my spirit, and close to my heart. I wanted to hold it with my whole self. A young Hawaiian came to life on the screen telling me that he was gifted, and that he had had the great good fortune to have been trained by island navigators and by an old astronomer. "Navigation is about both science and tradition," he said. "It is really very simple. That is, the theory is very simple. Putting it into practice is very hard. He can navigate," he said of his teacher, "by looking up." He then looked into the camera, serious and reflective. "We look down at our maps. He looks up at the sky, ahead to the horizon, around to the ocean swells and up to the flight paths of birds. He can see," he said. "in his mind he can see past the horizon. Over the horizon. He can see things others do not see."

"Taking risk allows us to seek new horizons and we all benefit from being horizon hunters." Thus spake the second man to walk on the moon, Buzz Aldrin, who by the way legally changed his name to Buzz in the 1980s.

We shall not cease from exploration.
And the end of all our exploring
Will be to arrive where we started
And to know the place for the first time.
— T. S. Eliot, *Four Quartets: Little Gidding*

DISAPPOINTMENT

Perhaps life is not a puzzle, after all, with pieces being handed to me one at a time to be turned over and checked for color, shape, and size. Will I finally recognize myself when I have put all the fragmented and separated pieces together? At the end of it all will I recognize the real me? Will I, too, see with trained and thoughtful eyes as I look up?

Or am I more like the little ocean fish that tapped an older fish on his left shoulder in order to ask timidly, "Excuse me, sir. You are older and wiser than I, and will probably be able to help me. Tell me this, where can I find this thing they call 'the ocean'? I have been searching for it everywhere." The older fish looked the youngster up and down with a fishy grin, placed a fatherly fin on the young fish's shoulder and, as gently as he could, replied, "The Ocean is what you are swimming in now."

"Oh, this?" said the young fish, feeling disappointed. "But this is only water! What I'm searching for is the ocean." And he swam away to search elsewhere.

DOWNSIDE UP

Or is it more like the time I took my trusty Merc down to Laguna for a checkup. My brake light needed fixing, but the most puzzling thing for me was that all of a sudden, I could not get my CD player to work. I had owned my car for some years and had much experience in loading the CDs into the trunk cavity. But suddenly there was no soothing music to help me glide peacefully up and down the southern Californian highways, and I missed it.

Mr. Helpful Merc Person pulled his head out of my trunk and stood up, trying unsuccessfully to cover his grin. He brushed a forelock away from his eyes and laughed at me, "You have put all your CDs in upside down."

"I can't be that stressed!" I laughed back at him. "You can, you know," he grinned.

WHISPERINGS

Will I gather the drooping skirts of my courage as the Italians settle down into the paper bag of my life, snickering quietly, thumping their foreheads with the heel of their hands and whispering, "*Capisce*?!" or "*Ma che vuoi*?" "Do you understand. But what the heck do you want?" Am I afraid? Afraid that without the Italian connection I will feel pedestrian, like having a Weetabix for breakfast?

EVERETT AND ME

I did once have the temerity to visit the office of a certain Michael Everett Capuano, who himself had the temerity not to be in. As a US Representative from Massachusetts from 1999 to 2019 and a Capuano to boot, I had hoped that he and I would quickly establish a grand connection. I had lived in both Rhode Island and Massachusetts in the States for seven wonderful years of my life, birthing three babes there, and this Michael Capuano was of Italian and Irish descent, as was I. I needed to meet him. I needed the connection. I needed to belong to some living and hopefully breathing remnant of the Capuano-Pavarno clan to which I still believed I belonged by dint of blood and genes, the nose, and the fact that Willis always proudly told all who would pay attention that I did look like Sophia Loren. "Didn't I?" he would challenge.

When I discovered that Sophia was a Neapolitan, I thought that maybe Willis was not wrong and that she and I were long-lost cousins. But as I never did meet her, I probably will never know. Trouble was, I could not work out how Willis even knew about Sophia Loren, as he did not attend the movies. The only thing I could think of that Sophia and I had in common was the fact that she and I both resisted buying rouge, instead daubing a little lipstick to our cheeks and rubbing it into submission.

But I did not meet Michael Capuano, and I could not tuck him into my paper bag of Italians.

At Michael Everett Capuano's office. But he was not in.

RUNNING INTO ITALIANS

In Providence, Rhode Island—in Salem, Massachusetts—in Beverly Farms, Massachusetts—in Fall River, Massachusetts—and in every other place I ever lived while back east in the States, I ran into Italians. They all sounded and acted very much like Americans to me, but again and again I was perplexed by their self-introduction, which went something like this: "Hi Jillian. I'm Pammie. I'm Italian." This last stated with a friendly grin. It puzzled me, and even more so when I met their parents or grandparents, most of whom had been born in America. But Italy was their proud heritage, and they wore it like a flag.

ORACLES I HAVE KNOWN

As I trekked the world with Mr. T, I stopped awhile here and there to consult with oracles of yore about the Italians in my paper bag of life.

I asked an ancient tree near the Amazon River. As it stood silent with the sound of the river rushing by, I was caused to ponder at the rushing in my life compared to the patience and stillness and quietness of the tree. And I remembered again that the book of Isaiah tells me that, "In quietness and confidence shall be your strength," or translated another way, "The Lord may calm your storm, but more often He'll calm you."

Consulting an ancient tree in the Amazon.

In Sweden I consulted with an ancient moose, patiently surveying the world from his place mounted on a wall. He appeared to reach toward me, but he, too, remained silent and unblinking despite all that he had suffered and all that he had endured and all that he had seen from his position stuck unmoving up there on the wall. And I pondered the strength of his quietness.

Consulting the patient moose in Sweden.

With a carved stone Moai, at least five-hundred years old.

In Hawaii's Polynesian Cultural Center in Laie, Oahu, I came upon a powerful, ancient, carved stone Moai—a monolithic human figure carved by the Rapa Nui people of Easter Island. The Moai had fascinated me ever since I had read of the adventures of the Norwegian ethnographer Thor Heyerdahl, who sailed from Peru in South America to the Polynesian islands. His historic journey across the Pacific Ocean was on the balsa-wood raft, Kon-Tiki, which he had built himself. He later did significant anthropological studies on Easter Island. The ancient Easter Island Moai are believed to represent the ancestors of the Rapa Nui people. That Moai and I had some quiet moments together, and as he, too, was silent I remembered again that in quietness and in confidence will be my strength.

Standing guard with Qin Shi Huang warriors.

Even the terracotta warriors depicting the armies of Qin Shi Huang, the first Emperor of China, which stand outside Xi'an, Shaanxi, China, remained implacable, unyielding, and unbending as they watched out for the approach of enemies from within or without. They had nothing to say to me about Italians—theirs, mine, or anyone else's. They had more than enough to do.

RABBI AND FRIENDS

I loved every minute of living in Orange County. It always made me laugh each time I drove north to visit friends in Los Angeles County, as they were astonished that anyone could have driven up the freeway from as far away as Orange County. There was often hesitation followed by a slow look of surprise as they endeavored to absorb the astonishing fact that a real live person from Orange County was standing right there in front of them. Los Angeles County was the center of the universe, was it not? It always had been, had it not? And Australia? What? Where?

A local Orange County rabbi honored me with an invitation to the Passover Seder in his home. As I was the only one of two Gentiles invited, I grasped the rare opportunity with both hands. Following the Seder plate of *matzah, zeroa,* egg, bitter herbs, *charoset* paste and *karpas*—and when we had a moment to relax—I asked the wise old men who were assembled if they could bring any of their wisdom to bear on my search for the Italians in my paper bag of life. One looked long and hard at me, came close to my side and said quietly, "You know, don't you?" That was all.

With the Rabbi Haim Asa of Temple Beth Tikvah and his wise friends.

GAETANO

Mr. T and I visited Capo d'Orlando, Catania, the Belvedere di Piraino, San Fratello, and Enna—then Agrigento and San Biagio Platani. Then again on to Agriturismo Casalicchio and the Castle of Mussomeli, Piana degli Albanesi, and Marsala, Bagheria, and Siracusa Ortigia.

Sicily is a part of Italy. I know that. A southern part and an island, but a part of the whole. I knew that before I met Gaetano. According to Gaetano, who has lived happily on the side of Mount Etna with his Finnish wife for many decades, "Sicily, Jillian, is Sicily," he said, grinning his huge all-embracing energy at me. He was not expecting me to argue with him, and he moved his hand quickly in a downward and dismissive motion as he turned and moved on with the next part of our exploration. And that, as we say, was that.

The Sicilian story—her people, her invasions, her earth-quakes, her recoveries, her rebuilding, her pain, and her loss—had filled my mind with fascination and wonder. A two-week journey back and forth across the island with Gaetano a few years earlier had only caused me to desire more, to know more, to experience more, to feel more, and to wonder again. I was anxious to learn at every step and to turn every corner into an adventure. The tenacity of the people who had met the turmoil of challenging centuries intrigued me. Phoenician, Carthaginian, Greek, Roman, Vandal, Ostrogoth, Byzantine Greek, Islamic, Norman, Aragonese, Spanish, and German influenced and sometimes controlled the island. My desire built up into action until Mr. T and I set off from Melbourne to crisscross Sicily with Gaetano one more time.

Gaetano is a wonder of a man. He conducts personalized tours with such energy and verve—such a deep knowledge of the food and wine, the history and privilege, the rocks and rills—that we were geared up and ready for everything he would reveal. As he drove us back and forth across the island for four triumphant weeks—talking, talking, and talking—his hands from time to time touched the wheel in between florid Sicilian gesticulation and explanation. He could answer every question we put to him. He could navigate the narrow streets and roads and lead us safely within a centimeter of the nearest car. He could stop at the most obscure of villages and show off the wonderful local produce. He could bring us to towns of devastating beauty. Devastating because "all the young people had left." Beauty because of the vistas. "You could purchase some of these homes for one dollar," he grimaced. "The young people have all left for the cities. Now there are only old people here." It was tempting.

Everywhere we went, the local businesspeople were delighted to welcome him and fuss over us. He had brought business right to their doorstep year after year for thirty years. And he was good company. He was funny, gregarious, hard-working, and even curious enough and passionate enough about history to own his very own ancient cave that he was furbishing as a place where he could get away.

TIGERS

The church bells rang out at 10:20 p.m. in Richmond town. This was so unusual that it gave me goose bumps. They often tolled their joy into all corners of Richmond in celebration of weddings, but not many weddings were held at 10:20 p.m. on a Saturday night. I thought for one moment that I was in Europe. Was I hearing the somber warning bells of war?

We were living through a season of unique challenges. Death stalked through the city on COVID legs.

COVID had sent the Tigers, our local Richmond football team, to temporarily relocate to Queensland, forced into playing far from their hometown.

With the medical officer determined to ensure the safety of the club, players, officials, and the community of Melbournians, there had been no other safe choice. Richmond's cheering fans could not fly to Queensland. There were no flights in and out of Melbourne town at all. The city of Melbourne and Richmond town were both awed into a strange silence in place of the normal revelry. It felt odd.

Gaetano Failla at the door to his very own cave.

The Richmond Tigers had moved up the ladder until they were set to play in the Grand Final—*and their fans could not attend?* It was a stark reminder of the seriousness of the virus. Coaches implored our players preparing in far north

Queensland to cast aside distractions, while supporters determined to remain proudly supportive from afar.

As I hopped into bed on the night of the Grand Final, the bells pealed out into the darkness of the night. Why? I took in a questioning breath and waited. The pealing went on and on, rising as a great wave to wash over the town of Richmond. It grew in intensity and reverberated from home to home, street to street, and lane to lane. It took me but one more breathless moment to realize that they were peals not of war but of joy. The Richmond Tigers had won the Grand Final! Far away in Queensland, 97,302 had watched the game. And we, so very far from the game, were blessed by the pealing of the great bells of the church of St. Ignatius's on Church Street. We joined in their exultation, carried on a wave of joy and celebration.

TIGERS IN TAORMINA

Far away in Sicily, as Gaetano drove us from Catania we pleasured in the joy of his effervescent company and our return to Sicily with four weeks of adventure ahead of us. His hands almost on the wheel, Gaetano welcomed and explained and gestured and effused as he steered us safely through streets and lanes, up and down hills, and around precipitous curves— as a camel through the eye of a needle.

As he gentled us expertly around one more curve, Gaetano pulled his car to a halt near the top of the small hill and turned to ask me in a voice both thoughtful and quiet, "Do you like music, Jillian?" I did. I do. "I have a friend in the next town you might like to meet. He is a musician. I will call him and see if he is at home."

Gaetano's friend was at home and willing to welcome unexpected visitors from Australia.

And so it was that we stepped through the back of the armoire of C. S. Lewis's *The Lion, The Witch and The Wardrobe*. Our musical adventure took us into the medieval house of Liuteria Severini, where he reconstructs fascinating musical instruments from prehistory to the Middle Ages. After one hour of historic wonder under the tutelage of this master teacher I was reluctant to leave, but more adventures awaited us.

Gaetano called a few days later. There was to be a concert in Messina at the Chiesa Santissima Annunziata dei Catalani, an ancient church known for its marvelous acoustics. Built on top of the ruins of an older temple dedicated to Neptune, it was constructed between the twelfth and thirteenth centuries in the Byzantine style with Arab-Norman influences and is partly buried due to rubble caused from the earthquake of 28 December 1908 that raised the road three meters. Here, Liuteria Severini and his wife were to perform with some of the historic instruments he had crafted. They were to be accompanied by a group of traditional singers. Would we like to come?

"I know a young sister who likes music also," mused Gaetano as we drove toward the church. "I will call and ask if she would like to join us. Would that be all right with you?" And thus, it was that five of us joined the group gathered in the only church in Sicily not to have been seriously damaged by the great earthquake of 1908. We were Gaetano, Mr. T and me, and the sister and her Superior, whom we had picked up at Casa Domus Nazarena on the apex of the hill in Taormina, where they resided looking out over one of the best views in Sicily. We basked in the glory of an improbable gathering in such an impossibly beautiful and ancient setting. It was hard to breathe for the glory and passion of it all.

After offering our gratitude to Severini and his wife and other performers, we moved from the church and its magic and followed Gaetano to the ice cream shop. As we moved along the *marciapiede*, still entranced, I continued in conversation with the younger of the sisters (who spoke very good English) while her superior smiled on, sweetly patient and nodding with approving grace.

Originally from the Philippines, the younger sister, Elvira, had had the opportunity to improve her English during her time living in Australia. Australia? Really? Oh yes, she had lived five years in Australia. Really? By now my eyebrows were arching toward the Sicilian skies.

Yes, she was moved to various parts of the world at the will of her order, and her five years in Australia had been a wonderful experience for her. She missed it still.

Did she know that Mr. T and I were from Australia? No, really? Where was it she had lived in Australia? "Do you know the older suburb of Richmond, which lies close to downtown Melbourne?" she asked, smiling at me through loving bites of Sicilian ice cream. Now it was my turn to draw in another breath of astonishment. Had Gaetano set this up?"Were you aware that Mr. T and I live in Richmond," I responded, quietly reluctant at the thought of a joke on me.

Severini and wife in concert in the Church of the Santissima Annunziata dei Catalani, Messina, Sicily.

"Do you know the Daughters of Divine Zeal in the Madre Nazarena Student's House on Church Street?" she replied through more licks of her ice cream.

I let out a breath of disbelieving air. "I do. We live a two-minute walk from there," I whispered. "When were you living there?" And then it tumbled out onto the marciapiede and bounced around for our disbelieving ears to hear—she had lived a two-minute walk from our Richmond home for five of the years Mr. T and I lived in Richmond. While Sister

Elvira was caring for female tertiary students from overseas, interstate, and country Victoria, Mr. T and I had been going about our business only one block away. How many times had I walked past that student's house during those five years? And she was a Richmond Tigers supporter? And we were in Taormina, Sicily? And we were meeting in this ancient Sicilian town after a medieval music concert in an ancient Sicilian church?

The Italians were in my paper bag everywhere I went. On this day I was enjoying a memorable concert in an ancient church, then licking an ice cream with a sister who, I was learning, had come originally from the Philippines and who had lived for five years nearly next door in Richmond, Victoria, Australia, and was now resident in a house on the top of a hill in Taormina, Sicily. And we were meeting by accident? Or was this by divine intervention?

A meeting In Taormina, Sicily, with Sister Elvira from the Philippines, who had lived two minutes from our Richmond home for five years.

And we had never met—until a medieval music concert in Messina, Sicily.

SICILY SERENADE

The four-weeks adventure crisscrossing Sicily with Gaetano was a joyful conglomeration of gastronomic delight, visual delight, and physical delight. When we thought we were all done, Gaetano grinned his Sicilian pleasure across a table to us as he promised one last feast. This one he was sure we would not believe. "Such produce! My friend! Andrea!" he gestured emphatically, tapping his broad chest to indicate the relationship.

The Ortigia food market in Siracusa was fragrant with produce and busy in a jostling pre-Covid kind of way, bustling with both noisy vendors and noisy buyers and resounding with much squabbling friendly trade. The lengthy queue waiting patiently for their food along the front and down the side of Andrea Borderi's business, Caseificio Borderi, was my first clue as to what might follow. After introductions, we were taken to sit at a communal table in the yard, as Andrea indicated with great conviction that he knew exactly what we would enjoy, and of course we did not need to order. We sat expectant, drinking in the life of the market as we watched from afar. Andrea, his wife, and his team plated enormous sandwiches succulent with such a variety of salads and cheeses and meats that we had to laugh. To our table he brought platters filled with small mountains of mouthwatering local produce, all carried with the reverence of an offering and placed before us with joy. I had never felt more Italian.

We indulged ourselves in the benevolence of Andrea's offerings over much good-natured banter, licked our lips and drained the last of our Chianti, and walked over to thank him. He smiled and bowed in the courtly Sicilian way, then smiled again as he tried to tell me something important in Italian, indicating that I should not depart just yet. "Stay! Stay!" Taking up a huge roll of paper towels, he stood at his workbench and he tore off sheet after sheet. I turned to thank him again and take my leave, but was waved back to stay "right there" and "see." He walked the whole length of the meandering queue of his hungry patrons gesturing to me, and handing each one a sheet of paper towel.

And then with him conducting and all present waving their paper towels, they began to sing. To me! They waved their paper towels to the rhythm of the music and the whole motley choir were laughing and singing and paying obeisance to me, a stranger in a foreign land.

There in the Ortigia Market they serenaded me with paper towels and laughter to the words of "Donna Senza Età" (Ageless woman). It was startling.

"Everything is normal here in Sicily," I was told. It does depend, I do believe, on whose eyes you are peering through.

Later, I sat in a Mauro café overlooking the water, drinking in both Etna wine and the smell of Sicily. A young man swaggered past me, dark-haired and gorgeous in an audaciously Italian way. As he passed by and the back of his T-shirt came into view, I read with pleasure, "Be Smile," written in bold letters.

With Andrea Borderi in Caseificio Borderi at the Ortigian Market, Siracusa.

MUSIC FOR THE SOUL

And I remembered that, twice before, a choir had been brought to sing to me. Few experiences have humbled me so. While in Houston, Texas, one year on business, a friend suggested that she would have a small luncheon for me the next time I came into town if I would like. I would like, and she did plan a small luncheon for me. When I arrived, I was confounded by the fact that there were more than two hundred people at that "small" luncheon, which was held in the best restaurant in town and that she had arranged for not one but two choirs to sing to me, after which I was expected to give a speech. I was rendered speechless. Well, almost. What a blessed gesture of generosity and love. Talk about, "Be smile."

In Houston it was a lovely friend who brought two choirs to sing to me, and at that point I could not have anticipated a serenade at the Ortigia Market in Siracusa years later thanks to a new friend. Andrea Borderi offered me fine food and wine along with the added free gift of music and laughter and shared joy.

Many years before, when I was staying outside the city of Lucca in northern Italy, it had been recommended that I take myself to a small local restaurant known as Florentino's. There, toward the end of a dinner of succulent baby lamb, I was serenaded by a group of local men who had been laboring all day on the stone walls that edged the sides of roads winding up the hill from Lucca. "*Cemento! Cemento!*" was the only word we had in common. They could see that I could understand the paragraph or two held within those two words.

As the Chianti flowed, two of the workmen began to sing. More and more of their weary compatriots joined in until the soft air of the night was filled with their harmonizing. Their faces were transformed from the masks of weariness that I had seen earlier into those of a choir of hard working but glowing Italian angels. At their invitation I, too, raised my voice and sang with them in Italian, lifted on the wings of their music. "O Sole Mio," we offered into that blessed Italian night, the Neapolitan song written in 1898.

> "Ma n'atu sole
> cchiù bello, oje ne'.
> O sole mio
> sta 'nfronte a te!
> O sole
> O sole mio
> sta 'nfronte a te!
> sta 'nfronte a te!

> But another sun,
> that's brighter still
> It's my own sun
> that's in your face!
> The sun, my own sun
> It's in your face!
> It's in your face!

"My Sunshine," we sang, "you are my sunshine…." I am warmed still by the sunshine that passes across my soul from all the generous folk who have brought the healing balm of their music, the fragrance of their food, and the generosity of their love to me without price, in Houston, in Sicily, and in Lucca—and in so many corners of the world.

PAPER NAPKIN IN LUCCA

We met on the island of Bermuda, where brightly painted houses punch out their jubilance as they stud the hillsides. We were both on retreat. We took one quick look at each other and said, "Want to go?" and we were out of there, into a cab and on our way to the water's edge to enjoy the cab driver's recommendation for the best restaurant in town. There we sat mellowing in the sunset, eating fresh lobster and drinking champagne over much laughter and the telling of Italian tales.

Dina was a true New Yorker. Born there of Italian immigrant parents, she filled my imagination with her tales of a New York pulsating with the daily dramas of immigrants who had melted into America through a porous border. Despite our many years' age difference, we shared a slightly zany sense of humor and both loved any opportunity for a good dose of storytelling. We had a jolly good time. Dina flew back to New York and I to Orange County. We kept up a correspondence, and each time I was in New York we took the opportunity to catch up to enjoy a meal and more tale-telling.

A few years after our Bermuda meeting, I was living back in Australia and married to Mr. T. I called Dina to let her know that we were preparing to travel to Italy, as I had determined to drag Mr. T off to the beautiful Lucca to see for himself what I loved about that place. Dina's daughter lived in Florence, and improbable as it seemed, Dina was planning to visit her during the same time period in which we would be in Lucca. Thrilled at this unexpected opportunity, we made plans to meet up in Florence.

Thus, it was that Mr. T and I caught the train from the walled Tuscan city of Lucca to Florence in order to meet up with Dina and meet her daughter and photographer husband for the first time. Everything about our lunch was filled with Florentine history, food, wine, and local stories. As we were preparing to bid our friends farewell, Dina's daughter turned to her husband to ask him if he could remember the name of a particular restaurant they had enjoyed, which was close to the walls of Lucca. He could not, so she resorted to a paper napkin on which she drew a ring that was to represent the walls of Lucca. Off to one side of this ring she drew a small cross. "I cannot remember its name," she apologized, "but it is there, just outside the walls," now pointing to the cross. "It should not be too hard to find."

Perhaps it would not be too hard for her, an Italian-speaking girl who had lived many years in the area. But for us, a snaffled white paper napkin with a circle and a small cross and no N, S, E or W, did not look too helpful. We thanked her anyway and took our train back to Lucca.

The old center of the city of Lucca is closed to traffic, and as it is a relatively flat city space, we did all our exploring on foot. With the Tuscan sun shining on our shoulders, we explored every nook and cranny until we decided to venture outside the city walls. Wandering along dirt tracks with grasses gentling in the breeze, with an historic old church on our left we passed a small sign on the right that stated simply, *Ristorante,* written on an arrow that appeared to be pointing toward the sky. As one who always desires to know what is on the other side of the mountain, I took Mr. T by the hand and urged him onwards and upwards and over the hill. And there was a restaurant. And that restaurant was the very one Dina's daughter had wanted us to find. And we had no map, and we had no directions, and here we were. And the food was amazing.

Following our meal, the maître-d' came to us proudly, smiling an all-gracious Italian smile, and offered us each a gift of tissue-paper thin slices of ham, a local delicacy of which he was very proud. The ham was folded onto a small plate, gently, like a fine linen handkerchief. "The pigs were fed on acorns," he said, smiling gently, sober and proud to be bringing us this offering. It tasted like acorn-flavored liquid gold. Italian gold.

PASTORI

Why do I tear up so, with deeply felt emotions for which I have no name?

I am standing on the side of a street in San Fratello, high up in the Sicilian highlands in the crown of the Nebrodi Mountains. Gaetano has navigated many hairpin turns without drawing breath or appearing to ever place his hands to the wheel, in order to offer us a visit to this remarkable town. Here we have seen the Giudei or Jews—sinister-looking soldiers from an army that never existed who gathered to disrupt the Easter celebrations in the town—wearing grotesquely masked faces and projecting madness. The masks worn over their faces were bright red, with circled black eyes. Some wore long tufts of white hair hanging down from one shoulder. Grotesque tongues hung out with studded silver crosses at their center. The disciplined drill of the celebration of Easter was solemn and powerful as hundreds of musicians marched past in slow rhythm to the music of the dirge. The Giudei mocked this solemnity with a deranged glee. A refined mixture of pagan and Catholic elements, the Good Friday Diavolata was a grotesque yet compelling festival.

I look up to see a group of older gray-haired gentlemen gathered on a balcony opposite me. They stoop slightly—in deference, in knowing, in recognition—respect passing between them with smiles. On the metal balcony railing a sign is mounted that reads, *Società Pastori*-San Fratello. It is a small and narrowly confined space. The single door-opening shadows whatever lies inside.

As I look across the street from where the celebration was held last night, the *pastori* take my breath down a notch, into a quiet and private place deep within my heart. "What does that mean?" I ask Gaetano in a whisper. I sense that there is something both infinitely precious and timeless here. He smiles, pleased that I have noticed. "They are shepherds, Jillian." He nods with quietly respectful reverence, "There are many shepherds in this area of Sicily."

And I am rendered speechless.

I hear the choirs of heaven singing, "And He shall lead His sheep," and my throat aches.

Società Pastori, San Fratello (Society of Shepherds).

The predominant work in this part of Sicily has always been that of shepherds.

ITALIAN LAMB

Mr. T and I were on a seven-day walking tour with a small group in Cinque Terra some years ago when it was recommended that it would be well worth our while to take a side trip to visit a particularly spectacular local vineyard. The next day we sat enjoying the quiet fragrance of the vineyard while sipping wine from the surrounding vines and chatting with the owner, who told us that he did not sell any of his wine but kept it all for family and friends. We relaxed in the afternoon sun as our conversation wended its way around the world to a discussion about life in Australia, a country of great interest to him. Oh yes, he had been there many times. Australia had been very good to him. For many years he had run a successful international business, exporting frozen Australian lamb to Saudi Arabia.

What a paradox. It seemed so unlikely to be sitting in a family-owned vineyard in this most Italian of settings and discovering that our host owned a business exporting of all things, frozen lamb out of Perth, Australia, to Saudi Arabia.

The Italians were in my paper bag everywhere I went.

CHIANTI KID

Casey and her husband were very welcoming to me when I arrived as the new kid on the block in Orange County. Roger was a well-regarded architect, and Casey was his energetic, creative wife—full of enough ideas and enough verve to keep him hopping. When Roger developed cancer, we all grieved, and it was excruciatingly painful to watch his demise. Casey never for one moment dropped the ball, moving all that needed to be moved to care for him and his needs and tend to the many friends who wished to visit and acknowledge Roger's contribution to society. As Casey cared for Roger throughout the harrowing months, my admiration for both of them grew and grew.

When Roger died, Casey and I spent more time together, often eating out, as is the Californian way. We shared trials and triumphs over meals of laughter and wine as we learned about each other's lives. One fine evening in a fine Italian restaurant that had been suggested for our evening repast, we settled in to another evening of remembering and laughing over the day's doings. It was time for fine wine. I asked our waiter if he kept a good Chianti in some hidden corner of his establishment. Casey was not familiar with Chianti but was more than ready to give it a go. I ordered a bottle. "I am sure that you will like it," I said. "It is a simple wine, easy on the palette." Casey was happy with that, and dinner was enjoyable. When the bill came, I took it, as I was sure it was my turn. But it was not my turn to keep a straight face when I looked at the bill, and I could not keep the indicator of shock from my face. I had not used my good common sense to ask the price of the Chianti before ordering it. In Australia Chianti was usually a reasonably priced wine. In Orange County it was not. I was floored. The cost was three times that of our food.

Casey read me in a minute and offered to split the bill, while I was mortified in a strangely childish way, as though I had been caught in a crime or misdemeanor. Never presume, I remembered. Here I was offered one more opportunity to learn that lesson. We laughed eventually and did split the bill, and the best I could offer Casey in return for my arrogance was that she should take home the half bottle that was left over.

I implore you to watch out for Italian wine when you order without asking the price.

When I was a young thing just beginning to grow into adulthood, I disliked any and all wine that was offered to me. Years later, I was to discover that I had always been offered a Chardonnay, which I do not like to this day, but at that time I thought that I simply did not like wine and could not understand why anyone would drink such strange-tasting stuff.

And then came one life-changing dinner I was invited to as the guest of a Parliamentarian in Sydney. I was seated on his right in the Parliamentary dining room, enjoying myself and playing lady when he offered me the wine list and asked me to choose the wine I would like to order with my dinner. "Thank you, no," I demurred, "I do not enjoy wine at all." He was satisfied with that and ordered red wine for himself, which was duly brought to the table with all the palaver attached to any good sommelier. My host took the cork and sniffed delicately, put his head back slightly, gazed heavenward smiling ruefully and said, "Wrong side of the hill."

I will always remember that wonderfully pontifical moment

as I will remember to ask for the wine list and check the price before I order.

Another transformative moment for me came a little later in the evening when my host invited me to enjoy sip of the red he had ordered. And I did. And everything in my life of sipping and supping changed forever.

MISSING THE MISSING

I desired a two-wheeler bike when I was eight years old. At that time the norm for Melbourne kids was to ride hither and yon all over Melbourne town on the weekends, unsupervised. I longed for my own bike so that I could join the throng. Malvern Star was the big brand name at the time and that is what I expected. Their first shop was opened in 1902 in Malvern only a short distance from 45b, and most of our neighborhood kids felt a distinct kinship with the brand.

What I received was a second-hand bicycle that had been painted by Willis with much love and a hand brush and offered to me with pride. I dared not demur. I understood the significance of the effort he had made. From then on, many a Saturday morning I would be up and dressed and off exploring my world before much of the neighborhood had stirred. But the famous brand name was missing on my bike, and the gap left a little sadness in my heart.

After some years of working in California I was so overworked, overused, overwrought, and overtired that I began to realize that the work had taken almost all of me at the same time as it had given me much. I was able to be financially independent and could create a new life. But something was missing.

Friend Rosie had her own bout with gaps when she found that important things cannot only be missing, but go missing. Requiring a double knee transplant, she had whizzed off to the best hospital she could find, suitcase in hand. Trouble was, when it came time for the scheduled surgery, her new knees had not arrived. The new knees were missing, and Rosie's surgery had to be put off until they were found. When the new knees arrived, the next day the surgeon took out her old ones and replaced them with the now-found new knees. By the time I was able to visit Rosie she was drugged up on a morphine pump with her new knees exercising away via a machine for the purpose of preventing blood clots, and I was left wondering what they had done with the old knees.

I have most often accepted my fate. But then one day I read that if I had been smarter, I could have exploited it. I had missed that part of my training and definitely needed to read up on exploitation. I once read that in Manhattan you always look both ways when running a red light. Is that exploitation? What else had I missed?

YEAR OF THE SPIDER

As I lived through my childhood years at 45b, every week or two Willis would entice me outside. Emboldened by the stiff brooms we held in our hands we would swipe away frantically at the multitudinous spider webs attached to fences and windowsills, downpipes and bricks, and anything else that lay within the spiders' cunning reach. Our determination endeavored to match that of the spiders' brilliant cunning, as each time Willis would remind me that this was The Year of the Spider, spluttering over that with his Richards giggle. We tried our darndest, but it was a near impossibility for us to detach every single sticky web from the cracks and crevices and high places. Then, when we were exhausted and were sitting on the back porch at the end of all our endeavors, it was a near impossibility for us to detach them from our brooms.

My years of living have been filled with sticky webs of learning that have attached to many parts of me and clung there with ferocious tenacity, until I have slowly begun to assimilate the reasons for their hold on me.

I am also slowly, but slowly, learning about the Italians who have clung to me all of my life, and cling to me still.

BRILLIANT AND WISE

Merle had learned to keep her head below the parapet of life and her light beneath a bushel. Not much discussion of the Italians went on at 45b, they were just "there"—in the food, in the name, in the air, whispering.

In California, Juan Carlos had asked me on our first formal meeting, "How are you doing?" He was compassionate and kindly in his elegant Argentinian way, concerned for my welfare as the new girl on the block. "I am fine," I chirped, happily denial-filled. "My wife cried for three years," he whispered, solemnly concerned for me. I had to learn to be wiser about my feelings. Facts are stubborn things, and he knew how hard it could be to settle into a new country where everything is to be learned and the whole paradigm is other. I needed a paradigm shift.

An angelic-faced Uber driver once introduced himself to me as Keanu. His name, he told me in answer to my question, means "breeze over a mountain." How wise, his parents. What a profound gift to a child. He knew who he was, and his heritage blessed him each time his name was spoken.

MATTRESS-POLICE

Victoria had a worrying problem when she was a little girl because she was puzzled by the tag attached to the mattress on her bed which admonished her with a strident voice, DO NOT REMOVE each time she changed her sheets. The tags frightened her. She worried quietly about them for years. She confided that well into her adult life she was afraid that the mattress-police would arrive imminently if she had the temerity to cut off even one annoying hanging tag. Reminds me a bit of hanging chads.

This memory causes me to ponder the DNA-police and their role. Will they come for me if I decide against their advice, that I do have Italians in the paper bag of my life? Will they arrest me and try me in the court for DNA-naysayers?

Will they punish me throughout eternity with their glaring looks and huffing and puffing over my recalcitrance?

I read once that there are people who never sing, and thus die with all their music still inside them. Well, I have made a determination that I will sing. I will sing about the rellies I never did have the good fortune to meet. I will sing about their tales of adventure as they crossed the oceans of the world to find new worlds fraught with antipathy to their needs, misunderstanding of their language, mispronunciation of their names—and yet promises of a new life, new loves—and if good fortune smiled on them, gold! I will feel the breath of hopes and dreams as I listen to their whispers down there in the paper bag of my life, and I will hug it to my chest with gratitude and thanksgiving that I, too, am a multicultural girl— Irish, English, Scottish, and Italian blended together to make me who I am.

An Australian girl am I, and like those of us who have come latterly to this shore, I am grateful. I will learn to exploit that which I have been given. No mattress-police for me.

A FUNNY THING

As I fussed and fumed about my dirth of Italian DNA, I surprised myself with a bubble of laughter when, at the very end of all the formal pages I had been sent, there was an insignificant looking note which whispered, "2 percent French." I was flabbergasted. La France? This miniscule drip of knowledge was new to me. Who? Where? What? Perhaps it was not the milkman after all. Were the DNA-masters trying to lighten my load of frustration? After four sloggingly hard years of studying French in high school I was sufficiently indoctrinated to haltingly wend my way through Parisian society on my visits. That is, I was, until the terrifying discovery that if I opened my mouth and asked a question in French, I would then be answered in French. Unintelligibly rapid French. It was too much for this girl. But the drop or two of French DNA was news indeed. Even *I* had not imagined this. It pleased me.

I was only just beginning to settle down with a smile about the possibility of some member of the French nobility playing havoc with the life of one of my forebears, when, voila! More news.

I opened my computer to find a kindly note from the kings and consorts of DNA-land. "Your ancestry results are now even more precise," they apologized via email, eyes averted. "As you know we're constantly evolving the technology and methods behind AncestryDNA. Using a combination of scientific expertise, the world's largest online consumer DNA database, and millions of family trees linked with DNA results, we're releasing the most precise DNA update yet." Then they added this exciting rider, "Don't be surprised if we are able to make more refinements to these regions in the future."

More refinements? How pleasing. They would have it right at last. This time the Italians would be tucked safely back where they belonged, in my paper bag of life. I was excited. "See your updated results," the DNA kings and queens cried in glee. I was like a little kid, all butterflies and joy. I would pluck my deflated balloon up from the ground. I would be able to settle myself down and get on with my life. I would rerecognize the "me" I had always thought I was. I would be a true part of that Italian mob, the Capuano-Pavarno lot in my paper bag of life.

WHAT WAS THAT YOU SAID?

It is amazing how one click on the keyboard of a computer can take the stuffing out of your morning.

> Ireland 41%
>
> England and Northwestern Europe 29%
>
> Scotland 28%
>
> Eastern Europe and Russia 2%

Russia? Did they say Russia? Now it was not only the Italian mob that had leaked out of my paper bag, but the French had made a dash for it as well. And the Russians had taken over their spot? Was it that hasty hug and kiss from the benevolent Mikhail Sergeyevich Gorbachev that did it? Did some of his DNA rub off with the photograph we had taken together? Was it because he had put his arm gently about my waist as we stood together, he, stern-faced—me, grinning? So who should I see about that? I listened again and felt I had heard a sigh of dismissal.

NOTHING CHANGES

While I was reeling my way through that email the DNA news went calmly on and on, not at all perturbed by my reaction.

"Don't worry," it said, "your DNA doesn't change. What changes is what we know about DNA, the amount of data we have, and the ways we can analyze it. When that leads to new discoveries, we update your results."

"Plus ça change, plus c'est la meme chose," stated French journalist and novelist Jean-Baptiste Alphonse Karr. "The more things change, the more they continue to be the same thing." I am the same thing as I always was. I think. But perhaps not.

It could be that I need another oracle, silent as death, unbending, unblinking, waiting patiently for me to sort it out myself. "You will know the truth and the truth will set you free." The book of Proverbs says that, "Happy is the man who finds wisdom, and the man who gains understanding." This I need to seek. Not Italians but wisdom.

WHERE ARE YOU FROM?

I worked in the field of Real Estate in Sydney for a few crazy years. Precious memories form in my mind as I recall meetings with Armenian clients. Every Armenian I met was the model of courtesy, generosity, kindness, and concern for the state of what they thought to be my undernourished, skinny, overworked, and overwrought body. I was invited into many of their homes and offered gifts of food to fatten my body and loving concern to feed my spirit. Refrigerators were often opened for me to choose the food I preferred. Then, as we sat discussing life and business, again and again I would be asked, "Where are you from?" Later would come a murmured, "You look a little Armenian." I did? At the time I knew little of the Armenians and the suffering they faced in 1915 during and following the collapse of the Ottoman Empire and the death and dispersion of millions. Yet there was often a person or two who would pat my face lovingly and look at me with gentle pity as they collected me to their Armenian bosom.

Touched by their gracious humanity, I wondered if they could sense my suffering as I agonized my way through the grief of the end of a twenty-seven-year marriage. I had sensed this unspoken connection in Los Angeles when I was invited to meet with a group of Jewish folk who had escaped Germany at the time of the Second World War. One gentleman, distinguished by his beautiful features, removed himself from his group to come to me. Looking into my eyes he said, "You know, don't you." I did.

STIFLING THE STIFLERS

I will not be stifled, even by Covid-19.

I will not be stifled by my DNA results.

I will not be trussed.

I will watch that safety does not become more important than growth.

I will learn again and again about integrity, forgiveness, trust, and dignity.

I will stay alert to the warning from Alfred Hitchcock about standing too close to the edge of the frame.

I will learn again and again to be both observant and insightful.

I will learn to listen and to interpret wisely that which I have observed.

I will respect my Italian ancestors, whether they appear in my DNA or not. I will honor them and be grateful. They have given me a lot of fun, and I am one of them by name and knowledge and loving choice, despite the kings and emperors of DNA-land.

I will remember that God has given me wit.

I do suspect that I am very much like the hairdresser I watched with a wry smile a few years ago. He was raving on and on to one of his clients about a particular hair product he was endeavoring to sell to her. "It comes from ...." he started in, searching for words. Then trying again, he began, "It feels like .... It is for .... It makes it feel more like ... well! ...." And at last, he was able to blurt out what he had wanted to say all along, "Hair! If you know what I mean." He ended with a frustrated flourish, hands dropping disconsolate to his side. I did.

That is the way I am with the Italians now. I come from ..., I feel more like ... well... Italian! Capisce?! Do you understand?

Even as I gently edge into a paradigm shift, I am aware that I do not need to convince anybody else. Not one soul cares. But I care. And I can be as Italian as I always was, as complex and complicated as I wish. I will settle down about all this and relax into enjoying those gesturing hands and whispering voices in the paper bag of my mind.

REMAINS

The Italians shall remain exactly where I had always thought they were, deep down in my soul, my heritage, my blood-line, and my DNA. They are a bit of an ugly-looking lot if the few photographs I have are anything to go by, but unless the mattress-police or the DNA-police come searching, they will continue to hide and watch, to sing and dance and laugh and share succulent food and superb wine as they whisper their way on down through the years in the paper bag of my life.

I heard a wonderfully accomplished and very funny Italian musician introducing himself to his audience with a grand flourish. "Italians are the best in the world at expressing pain, misery, tragedy, the dramatic, and suffering." Here he paused for effect and laughter. Then he continued, "That is, they are the best in the world after the Greeks!"

It was blowing an arctic gale one day as I wandered one of the grungier of Richmond's streets, when a sudden juddering stop of revelation pulled me aside. Is it possible that I have been asking the wrong questions all this time? A shadow of a memory crossed my path, winking as it scurried away. One more time I smiled at myself.

Determined to satisfy my need for some free time and a dram or two of culture while living in Southern California, I turned to an acquaintance, then to a neighbor and then to a colleague. Was it my Aussie accent or my language that caused the looks of incomprehension I received? Forced to take stock of my efforts at expression, I refashioned my entreaties from, "Can you tell me where the art house movie theatres are in this part of southern California?" to "Are there any art house theatres in this part of California? Faces had looked up at me, puzzled, perplexed, and probing—but not hopeful. "Sorry. No." This always offered with a reluctant look of bewilderment. Frustration and need led me relentlessly on and into the reformation of my query and the refashioning of my language. "Can you tell me which movie theatres screen foreign films here in southern California?" I asked at last. No puzzled or perplexed or probing looks this time. "Oh," came the enlightened reply, "we don't have Mexican films here."

And one more time, that was the end of that.

GOODBYE, MY LOVE

The author Angie Thomas wrote, "Goodbyes hurt the most when the other person is already gone." And so it is at the end of my tale, as with all long-lost loves, I bid a sad farewell to the Italians who are not in my DNA, not with me as I thought they were, not committed to me as I was committed to them, but who continue to quietly chatter and laugh in the paper bag of my life. And I will find joy in their whispers. "Capisce?" they enjoin me. "Do you understand?"And I bend my head in acknowledgement. "I do. Oh yes, I do."

The heritage that had been an unquestioned part of my very existence has been brought into question. I study them well and defer to the fact that my Italians are not a lifeline, nor are they my ticket to anything. They are modest folk. There is neither pomp nor power there. And I am not bound to be a servant of my DNA as much as I lack the ability to change it.

The world of the Italians behind me is not screened off from my pleasure and joy at all they have brought to my table. They have hosted me with open arms and open hearts.

My response to the genome leaves me as my own master-piece, undeterred by the DNA-gurus to whom I gave consent to analyze parts of me I cannot see. They have neither magnified nor distorted. They cannot make an Italian of me. I am who I am with or without them, their opinions and their analysis. But neither can I cut the thread. I am attached by a silken spider thread to all things Italian—the men, the shoes, the art, the history, the clothes, the whole fascinating country.

The rich vestments of the lives of the Italians in my paper bag gleam their burnished light into my soul, and I am blessed.

I came so close to being Italian.

I will take the Italians I never met yet thought I knew and tuck them carefully into my paper bag of life. I will keep them safe and carry them with me like a little lunch box full of surprises. I will not let it go.

TUNING UP

Thelonious Monk, the American jazz pianist and composer, famously remarked, "The piano ain't got no wrong notes."

Italian or not. Neither do I.

THE SOUND OF SUNSHINE

Arnold Orville Beckman, chemist, inventor, investor, and philanthropist celebrated his hundredth birthday on 10 April 2000. At that time, he said, "Don't take yourself too seriously. Practice moderation in all things, including moderation." The American actress Lauren Bacall said in an interview, "If you don't make me laugh, I don't want to know you," and W. H. Auden is quoted in *The Dyer's Hand* as saying, "Among those whom I like or admire, I can find no common denominator, but among those whom I love, I can: all of them can make me laugh."

I cover my mouth and laugh quietly, acknowledging that I am a little like the slim package of ocean trout I opened recently. In bold print right beneath the word "Ingredients" it stated, "Contains fish."

LAUNCH PADS

Buzz Aldrin whispers to all who will hear and understand, that sunshine and launch pads are two of his favorite things. There is the sunshine again, just as brave and powerfully life-giving as it is when John Denver sings from his heart on a CD I have, which is as old as time, "Sunshine on My Shoulders Makes Me Happy." The Italians whisper to me, "*Luce del sol*," and there it is, life-giving and caressing my shoulders back into the place where they belong, up against the wall as I hold my back straight, ready for anything.

And launch pads? I listen closely to this talk as I adjust and readjust to the changes which continue to blow into my life, now on whirlwinds, now on a zephyr breeze, swirling away the old and bringing arms-full of surprises.

Buzz also has said, "There is nothing like gazing out the window while you're on your way to the moon." I say, "There is nothing like gazing out the window when you are whirled into a new adventure, learning again how to breathe, in and out, in and out—and learning how to think in a whole new world."

"One of the keys to success in life," Buzz tweets: "Always be ready when the right opportunity comes along."

We will meet again, my Italian ancestors and I. There will be birds and music and wine and laughter and good friends and gentle hugs and memories—and if we are blessed with great good fortune, those we have loved and lost will join us in joyous celebration.

During these Covid days I have found corners to clean that have not seen the light of day for a century or two.

I washed white towels with one teeny tiny G-string.

The G-string was red.

I did not want pink towels.

And I have pondered the lives of the Italians in my paper bag.

When my sons set their sights on overseas for the first time, I encouraged them not to panic if they missed a plane. Along the way I had learned, "There is always another plane."

And so I remind myself as I set out into my next new life, "There is always another plane."

That is, until there isn't.

So there!

ACKNOWLEGMENTS

My gratitude goes out to the many folk who have nourished me with wisdom and insight, encouragement and gentle direction.

Mr. T has been patience personified as I have spread papers far past the reaches of our dining room table. He has listened with discerning ears and commented with grace.

My beloved boys, Luke Benjamin and Toby John have encouraged and supported me every step of the way, as they do in all of my life.

Theresa Geissler, who laughed and cried with me as she listened patiently to drafts of section after section while tending to my nails.

Colin Rolfe of Epigraph, who has encouraged and directed me with care.

Dory Mayo, who has been a close and engaging editor as we have navigated both the pandemic and our Italian connections.

Kira Rosner, who has offered her warm and kindly encouragement for which I am grateful.

All have been key participants in the birth of my books.

And from afar and yet not so far at all, the beloved Bob Danzig has guided and encouraged my hand.

www.ingramcontent.com/pod-product-compliance
Lightning Source LLC
Chambersburg PA
CBHW031840090426
42741CB00005B/300